Conflict
Resolution
and Peer
Mediation

Conflict Resolution and Peer Mediation

Carolyn Simpson

ROSEN PUBLISHING GROUP, INC./NEW YORK

Acknowledgments

Many thanks to Elizabeth Richards of the National Resource Center for Youth Services (Tulsa, OK) and to Jean Anderson of the New Mexico Center for Dispute Resolution. Their materials on conflict resolution were immensely helpful in writing this book.

Thanks, also, to my editor Erica Smith, who has helped to make this a better book.

And, of course, special thanks to Dwain for his insight into interpersonal conflict and his willingness to hang in there and resolve "one more round."

Published in 1998 by The Rosen Publishing Group, Inc.
29 East 21st Street, New York, NY 10010

First Edition

Library of Congress Cataloging-in-Publication Data
Simpson, Carolyn.
    Coping through conflict resolution and peer mediation /
        Carolyn Simpson.
        p.   cm. — (Coping)
    Includes bibliographical references and index.
    ISBN 0-8239-2076-3 (lib. bdg.)
    1. Conflict management. 2. Interpersonal conflict in
adolescence. 3. Interpersonal communication in adolescence.
4. Mediation. 5. Peer counseling of students.
    I. Title. II. Series.
    HM136.S637   1998
    303.6'9—dc21   98-25246
                                                          CIP
                                                           AC

Manufactured in the United States of America

Contents

Introduction   1

PART I   THE NATURE OF CONFLICT   5

1   When Conflict Arises   6

2   Why Use Conflict Resolution?   17

PART II   HANDLING CONFLICT CREATIVELY   27

3   Problem-Solving Skills   28

4   Putting Your Skills to Work   44

PART III   USING PEER MEDIATION   66

5   When Do You Need Peer Mediation?   67

6   What Happens in a Peer Mediation Session?   75

Conclusion: Affecting the Outcome   83

Glossary   89

Where to Go for Help   91

For Further Reading   92

Index   94

A B O U T   T H E   A U T H O R ◇

Carolyn Simpson is an outpatient therapist at Family Mental Health Center, a division of Parkside, Inc., in Tulsa, OK. She also is a psychology instructor who designed and currently teaches a course on conflict resolution and mediation skills at Tulsa Community College.

Ms. Simpson received a bachelor's degree in sociology from Colby College, Waterville, Maine, and a master's degree in human relations from the University of Oklahoma. She has worked as a clinical social worker, school counselor, teacher and therapist. In addition, she has written more than twenty books on health-related subjects and career opportunities.

She lives with her husband and their three children in the outskirts of Tulsa. In her spare time, she coaches her daughter's league champion soccer team.

Introduction

Two children are fighting over a toy.

"It's mine. Give it back!" the girl yells.

"Mom said we're supposed to share!" the boy yells back.

"Well, I want it now. I'll share later." The girl tries to grab the toy out of the boy's hands.

"No!" the boy screams. "I'm playing with it now." He tries to hang onto the toy.

"Give it back," the girl screams, yanking on it.

The two children tug back and forth on the toy. Finally the boy lets go and the girl rolls backward, still clutching the toy. She hits her head on the floor. The boy laughs.

Suddenly the girl lunges at him and whacks him on the head. "Quit laughing," she says.

The boy rubs his head. "I'm telling Mom," he says, and he runs out of the room hollering, "Mom, Donna hit me."

Okay, so maybe you don't fight with your brother and sister over toys anymore. And maybe you don't run to Mom every time you don't get your way. All the same, you may use similar tactics as your way of dealing with conflict.

WHAT IS CONFLICT?

The dictionary defines conflict as an antagonistic state resulting from differing, often opposing, points of view or needs. The word "antagonistic" suggests that conflict is an

1

unpleasant condition, but that doesn't have to be the case. We can view conflicts as challenges and opportunities to grow if we handle them as such.

Conflict erupts over three basic issues: conflicting resources, such as land or material goods; conflicting psychological needs, for control, recognition, a sense of belonging, economic well-being and security; and conflicting values, which involve people's deeply held beliefs. Many conflicts are a combination of all three issues, which make them more complex and trickier to resolve.

As an example, consider the opening scenario. It is more than just a conflict about resources (the toy they both want). It can be just as much a conflict over psychological needs; the girl wants to control what belongs to her, and the boy wants to prove he has equal access. The conflict also contains elements of conflicting values: sharing and private ownership. The wise problem-solver learns to consider all elements of a conflict. You can learn skills to help you not only resolve your conflicts, but benefit from the experience as well.

CONFLICT RESOLUTION AND PEER MEDIATION

Conflict resolution is an approach to solving conflict that focuses on identifying and satisfying people's needs in order to come to a solution that's good for everyone. It requires the important skills of active listening and assertive communication. These skills carry over into all aspects of people's lives. The smaller conflicts we face every day in our families, school, and community merely mirror the larger conflicts that afflict organizations and countries. The same skills apply to solving both large and small conflicts.

Mediation means intervention by a third party (neutral person brought in from the outside) to settle a conflict that the participants have been unable to resolve on their own. Mediators don't force a solution or mandate one; they simply assist the participants by modeling their own conflict resolution techniques. That way, the participants arrive at their own solution as well as develop skills they can use again to resolve conflict.

Peer mediation is another conflict resolution strategy. In this case, the neutral third party is also a peer. He or she has no more authority than the participants themselves. However, he understands how to listen effectively, how to brainstorm solutions, and how to communicate assertively with others.

If you think of all conflict existing on a continuum, problem-solving lies toward the left where you have the most power to influence the outcome. Arbitration (a third party has the authority to mandate the solution) and the courts lie on the right where you have the least power to influence the outcome. Mediation falls somewhere in-between.

```
___ /_____ /_____ /_____ /_____ /_____ /__
problem-   formal       peer         mediation   arbitra-   the
solving    negotiation  mediation                tion       courts

(Most power                                      (Least power
to influence                                      to influence
outcome)                                              outcome)
```

WHAT YOU WILL FIND IN THIS BOOK

This book will provide you the skills to handle different kinds of conflict. You will learn how to listen more effectively, how to make use of nonverbal behavior (because it's often not what we say, but how we say it that gets us in trouble), how to think creatively, and how to seek solutions that will satisfy all parties concerned.

In addition, you'll learn how to mediate other people's conflicts, building on the problem-solving skills you've already learned. You'll learn the importance of a peer mediation program and how to start one at your own school. Many schools are instituting peer mediation programs in the lower grades, in the hope that when students learn these conflict resolution skills at an early age, they will use them in other circumstances as they grow.

Once you've learned these skills, you'll discover that they are useful in settling conflict in a variety of situations: in school, at your workplace, and in your family.

There's no set way to solve a conflict, but there are certain guidelines. This book explores specific problem-solving skills.

PART ◇ I

THE NATURE
OF CONFLICT

CHAPTER 1

When Conflict Arises

C onflict is an inevitable part of life. Unfortunately, violence often erupts out of conflict, as can be seen from significant events in history. War has been around since the dawn of humanity, resulting from differences concerning ideals, land, or religion. Consider the ancient Romans, who created an empire regardless of what the conquered peoples wanted. Modern-day conflicts in Bosnia-Herzegovina, Northern Ireland, the Middle East, or the Russian republics, especially Chechnya, are more modern examples of struggle.

As you hear about them on television or read about them in history books, these conflicts may seem entirely different from those you encounter every day. But when you look more closely, you can see that large-scale conflicts often are based on the same principles, and follow the same patterns, as the smaller ones you encounter in your daily life.

For example, the situation in the Middle East shows how a single conflict is usually not one single "type," but is a mix of the different elements we discussed in the Introduction. Here, the Israelis and Palestinians have been in conflict over a shared homeland for the greater part of this century (the nation of Israel was created out of Palestine in 1948 as a place for Jewish people to settle after World War II). While this is first a conflict over *resources* (land), it involves *values* as well—in this case, religious values, since Israel and Palestine are home to people who are Jewish, Christian, and Muslim. And as Israelis and Palestinians both desire a homeland, each group has certain *psychological needs*: the Palestinians want independence from the Israeli state, and the Israelis want a nation of their own.

But you don't have to look always at the history books or watch the evening news to see or feel conflict around you. If you have witnessed how gangs operate, you have seen how gang life often imitates the world at large. Conflicts start out over turf (resources) because the ability to defend your turf shows others how powerful you are (a psychological need). If one group burns another, retaliation becomes the only way to save face. Violence begets more violence.

Family life also presents its own unique conflicts, since you often have a houseful of people with different needs and agendas.

Sometimes, it's just a matter of different expectations. Your parents want you to grow up to be a doctor. You, on the other hand, don't want to go to college at all, let alone to medical school. If you don't try to live up to their expectations, they will resent it. If you do try to meet their expectations when it's not what you want, your conflict festers inside you. Conflict is also common when families have to adapt to new circumstances, such as birth, illness, or death. Divorce and abuse can complicate the picture.

If you have a job, you probably already know that you are likely to encounter conflict there as well. Maybe you have too many responsibilities and not enough pay, or maybe you just don't see eye-to-eye with your boss. Jobs are hard to find; it isn't wise just to walk out when you encounter a little conflict. It is much wiser to try to resolve the conflict amicably.

TYPES OF CONFLICT

While there are three ingredients to conflict, there are four actual types of conflicts.

Intrapersonal conflict is the type of conflict that arises from within yourself. Think of it as a dilemma, a conflict resulting from guilt, or a conflict between your "real" self and the "ideal" picture you have of yourself.

Interpersonal conflict occurs between two or more people. As explained in the Introduction, interpersonal conflict usually erupts over differing beliefs, psychological needs, and/or resources.

Intragroup conflict arises within the context of a larger group but takes place between two or more people. For example, people working together in support of a political candidate may differ about the ways they want to run the campaign. The conflict is interpersonal (in that it's between two or more people), but it's also a part of a single, larger group. Intragroup conflict is complex to solve because it's not merely a matter of satisfying the needs of the two participants; you additionally are affecting all the other members of this particular group.

Intergroup conflict arises out of conflict between two or more groups. Gang warfare is a good example of intergroup conflict. In this case, the participants of one group are unified in their opposition with another group.

ELEMENTS OF CONFLICT

Wrong assumptions and misperceptions are responsible for starting many conflicts. When you don't understand the motives or behavior of another group of people, you may resort to stereotypes to explain their actions. Of course, relying on stereotypes (thinking everyone with a certain group affiliation is the same) does nothing to explain what that particular party is thinking.

Certain lifestyles are hard for some people to accept, especially a lifestyle that appears drastically different from their own. The problem is that many people base their assumptions about others on how they look. What we convey about ourselves through the clothes we wear, the car we drive, the type of house we own, our hairstyles, or our accessories, is very misleading.

For example, my husband wears an earring in his left ear, likes to wear jeans and sandals, and is saving up to buy a Harley. However, when he dresses for work (considering the suit and tie, not the tiny hoop earring), he looks starched and stuffy. People who have seen him at work assume he's a conservative Republican. People who see him around the house think he's a flaming liberal. Actually, he's a little of both, but no one would guess that from appearances alone.

Extend this argument to concern a person's sexual orientation, race, religion, class, and gender. Once someone has his or her own preconceived ideas of how someone will act, it is difficult to adjust the ideas when faced with contradictions. Consequently, people are afraid of situations they don't understand.

Because we don't take the time to understand the beliefs, needs, and motives of the person with whom we differ, we end up making wrong assumptions and misperceiving their intentions. In the end, the wrong assumptions and misperceptions contribute more to the conflict than the actual differences.

Communication style also affects conflict. Listening to someone who thinks differently from you and conveying what is bothering you are important to solving conflicts. Poor communication, which can result from not understanding your own feelings and needs, contributes to conflict. An example of this would be when someone chooses to be silent when he wants to convey how unhappy he is about something you've done or not done.

Finally, people increase the likelihood of conflict when they adopt an unyielding position. If I'm determined that the *only* way I'm going to pass geometry is by switching teachers, I've already discounted other arguments without even hearing them and am set on one particular course of action. If the school can accommodate my request, the conflict may or may not go away. (What if I just can't understand geometry no matter who is teaching me the subject?) If the school refuses or is unable to grant my request, the conflict is unsolvable because I've only considered one way to fix it.

HOW WE REACT TO CONFLICT/STYLES AND TACTICS

There's more than one way to handle a conflict. In fact, there are six ways to handle one, and one method will be preferable to another depending on the circumstances.

Avoidance

Avoidance as a tactic can be either positive or negative. Some situations don't warrant the time and energy spent working on a solution because they're not that important in the long run.

For example, every spring the garden bed of our front yard consists solely of dirt. To our neighborhood cats, it resembles one gigantic litter box. Each morning for weeks on end, we open our front door only to discover a fresh pile of cat droppings in the garden bed. When it first happened, I wanted to dig up the mess and drop it on our neighbor's front steps. I thought of calling them up and letting them have it about their stupid cats.

However, in the interest of being good neighbors, I chose to avoid conflict. In particular, I remembered when some of the homes in our neighborhood were being robbed—which worried us because my husband and I both worked away from home during the day. The woman next door with the wandering cats had called us and volunteered to keep an eye on our house, since she was home during the day. In this case, a squabble over her cats roaming in our garden was less important than keeping the goodwill of our neighbors.

Of course, there's a downside to avoiding conflict. For example, when Stacy got a car for her birthday, she offered her friend Michelle a ride home each day from school. After a few days, more and more people got invited to ride in Stacy's car. Eventually, Michelle discovered that Stacy no longer had room in her car for her. Michelle was angry because Stacy had more or less said that she'd always give Michelle a ride. After all, they were good friends and shared a lunch period. However, Michelle wanted to avoid upsetting her friend, even though she was terribly upset herself. So, she didn't say anything about not riding with Stacy anymore. But she was still angry. It got harder and harder to eat lunch with Stacy because she couldn't figure out why Stacy hadn't noticed she was hurt. What started out as a conflict over the rides home ended with Michelle avoiding Stacy altogether. They stopped eating lunch together; they stopped being friends. Avoiding dealing directly with the conflict made it worse.

It's important to remember that avoidance is a good tactic when the issue is not that significant to either of you. It's a bad choice when you are avoiding simply because you're afraid of the consequences or others' reactions.

Denial

Denial is more intense than avoidance, since it means not even recognizing that a conflict exists. Denial is rarely a useful tactic—you often end up deceiving yourself as well as others. Consider Jay and Cody.

Jay is overweight, and his classmate Cody teases him about it. Jay pretends it doesn't bother him, but he really dreads going to history class because of Cody's teasing. Since it actually is a problem, Jay's denial does nothing to diminish the conflict. Jay grows more and more upset about Cody and eventually drops that particular class, although that was his favorite teacher. In this case, denying a particular conflict made it grow.

People who deny a conflict also can end up displacing it (taking their anger out onto others). For example, Diana is mad at her boyfriend Matt for fooling around with a girl in his French class. She doesn't want to make a scene, though, so she pretends she isn't mad. Of course, she's still mad; she just can't express it toward Matt. When she gets home that night, and her mother asks her to help with the dishes, Diana blows up at her mom for making so many demands on her. Diana's anger with her boyfriend is being displaced, or spilling, onto her mother.

Accommodation

Accommodating is giving in, going along with the wishes of the other party even when you don't want to. Like other ways of dealing with conflict, it can be either positive or negative.

For example, Josh was supposed to visit his grandmother before going out with the guys Saturday night. The only problem was that his grandmother strongly disapproved of the way he dressed around his friends. She particularly disliked the earring he wore in his left ear.

"Look, why don't you take your regular clothes with you, leave them in the car, and wear something more dressy for your grandmother," his father suggested.

"That's such a pain," Josh said. "Why can't Grandma just accept me the way I am?"

"I wish she could," his dad said. "But she's set in her ways, and it doesn't really hurt you to take your earring out and leave it in the car, does it?"

"No, I guess it doesn't. I can change my clothes before we go."

Josh has accommodated his grandmother's wishes, even though that presented a conflict for him.

However, accommodating can simply be a way to avoid dealing with conflict. If you view conflict as something to be avoided at all costs, you may decide to give in to others.

For example, Jamie and her boyfriend were discussing where to go eat Friday night. Richard preferred Mexican, but Jamie had trouble eating spicy food. She suggested steak. When Richard turned his nose up at her idea, she assumed it was because steak was too expensive. Afraid that he might call off the date, she went along with his suggestion to eat Mexican.

However, an hour after they'd finished their spicy Mexican meal, Jamie's stomach began to act up. She was miserable, and had to ask Richard to take her home. He assumed she was making a statement about his choice of restaurant. He took her home and then went out to a local club looking for other company.

It is wise not to accommodate on issues that are significant to you. Giving in is only a useful tactic when you're not going to suffer serious physical or emotional consequences as a result.

Aggression

Launching an attack usually is not productive—it does little to preserve a relationship. That's the meaning behind the phrase "winning the battle, and losing the war." If you use aggression to force someone into going along with your idea, you may win that particular conflict, but lose your friend in the process.

People who resort to aggression do not have a positive view of conflict. More than likely, they think of conflict as a contest where there can be only one winner. Or they think of conflict as a struggle between two sides, and only their side is the right one. An aggressive person is most likely afraid to listen to the other side because he might not be able to control the outcome, and attempts to take control of the situation by forcing his will onto others. He may also be afraid of someone thinking he is wrong.

Compromise

Compromise is an effective way to resolve a conflict, but only if you are prepared to have some, not all, of your needs met. Consider the classic example of two family members arguing about the last orange in the fruit bowl. Both want it. Neither will give in to the other, so they decide to compromise and cut the one orange in half. The boy gets to eat only half the orange; his mother gets only half an orange to use in her recipe.

However, if the boy and his mother had better communicated their needs, they both could have gotten exactly what they wanted. The boy wanted to eat the fruit and all his mother needed for the recipe was the peel. Compromising only got them half of what they wanted.

Collaboration

Collaboration is the best way to solve a conflict and preserve a relationship. When you collaborate on a solution, you sit down with someone and treat each other as partners in the problem. You have to listen to each other in order to define the problem and clarify what each party's interests are. You learn to brainstorm different options that might help you two meet all of your needs. Instead of compromising, the boy and his mother could have collaborated. They might have sat down and considered the problem: both wanted the orange. However, more specifically, the boy wanted the fruit, and his mother wanted the peel. Knowing each person's real needs would have helped them to solve their dilemma.

If collaborating is such a positive way to deal with conflict, why wouldn't you use this method all the time?

Think about the time and energy involved in sitting down to hammer out a solution. If you collaborated on every conflict you encountered, you wouldn't have time for the rest of your activities. Collaboration is best saved for the important issues and the relationships that matter most to you.

CHAPTER 2

Why Use Conflict Resolution?

I f you watch the news, you're aware that the alternatives to problem-solving can escalate violence. People in warring countries match violent acts with more violent acts. Gang shootings often result in retaliatory acts by surviving gang members. Terrorism is aggression taken to its extreme.

The problem with this kind of tactic is that conflict becomes a struggle in which only one side prevails, and the underlying causes are not addressed or resolved.

American society is too quick to solve its problems with weapons. Weapons have long been called the great equalizers. A person who feels otherwise powerless can pick up a gun, and suddenly everyone bends to his will.

For example, kids who rely on guns and knives to settle their scores make their schools unsafe environments for learning. Metal detectors can try to stem the tide of weapons in the hallways, but they do nothing to teach students better ways to settle their differences. The answer isn't simply to take away the weapons, but to give people the skills and knowledge to resolve conflict peacefully.

Conflict resolution is more effective than violence because it lets people talk out all of their problems and needs. Both sides are heard and understood. Also, by having an active role in solving the problem, people feel empowered, and committed to honoring the outcome.

THE BEGINNINGS OF CONFLICT RESOLUTION

The problem-solving skills outlined in this book have a long history. Most recently, they are a result of the peace movement of this century. A major reason for the peace movement was the development of nuclear warfare. Since the United States first dropped them on Hiroshima and Nagasaki during World War II, nuclear bombs had become increasingly powerful weapons. People were frightened that the next war would mean nuclear war, and organized many protests. A popular slogan was "no nukes." Looking for peaceful solutions had become a critical issue—civilization was hanging in the balance.

The nuclear threat also created a great deal of tension among world leaders not to upset a balance of power. This period, from the end of World War II in 1945 to the fall of the Berlin Wall in 1990, is known as the Cold War. The United States and Soviet Union were the major players, and they were under pressure to work out their differences through negotiation rather than through war. However, their relationship was strained and they remained suspicious of each other. What's more, each country continued to build its arsenal of nuclear weapons, thinking that the threat of such devastating war would actually promote peace. While nuclear war did not erupt, other wars *did* erupt which represented the superpowers' international interests, namely in Korea and Vietnam.

Ironically, the Vietnam War was another event that mobilized the peace movement. People in the United States, particularly young people, felt that the war was unjust—they organized protests, sit-ins, and other nonviolent tactics to try to bring an end to it. Protesters had learned these tactics from the civil rights movement, particularly from the lives of Mahatma Gandhi and Dr. Martin Luther King, Jr.

Two of the great spirits of this century, Mahatma Gandhi and Dr. Martin Luther King, Jr., were famous for putting principles of nonviolence into action. They were concerned with protesting social injustices in their home countries. While this was not easy, and put them squarely in danger, these men succeeded in bringing about social change. Because they are so important in history, we will look at their lives and work in detail here.

Mahatma Gandhi

Mohandas Gandhi (it was not until much later that he was called Mahatma, which means "Great Soul") was born and educated in India. He studied an additional three years in England to become a lawyer. As a young man in his twenties, Gandhi went to South Africa to practice law on behalf of some Muslim businessmen. Gandhi had been there less than a week when he was thrown off a train for refusing to leave the first-class compartments, which were reserved for whites. Since Gandhi had purchased a first-class ticket as required, he intended to ride in the first-class compartment, as everyone else (who was white) did. Again and again, he was refused a seat. Shocked at the discrimination his Indian people faced in South Africa, Gandhi turned to the teachings of nonviolent resistance to protest the unfair laws.

Indians (called "coloreds") were restricted from voting, obtaining business licenses, or owning land. Gandhi filed suits on their behalf. When those efforts proved ineffective, he organized protests. Though he had finished his case for the Muslim businessmen a year after his arrival, he remained in South Africa another twenty-one years to help his people fight discrimination. In 1907 the British passed the Black Act, a law requiring Indians to be fingerprinted and registered. Indians then had to carry registration papers with them at all times or face arrest and/or deportation. Gandhi refused to comply with such a humiliating practice; he didn't register, and thousands followed his example. When a British official promised to change the law if Gandhi would only comply first, Gandhi demonstrated his trust by being fingerprinted and registered. When the official reneged on his promise to overturn the law, Gandhi (and many of his followers) staged a huge bonfire, where they destroyed all their registration papers. Gandhi was jailed for this act.

In the years to come, Gandhi was jailed repeatedly for protesting government policies, but in the end he succeeded in gaining better treatment for his people.

In 1915 Gandhi returned with his family to India. At first he devoted himself to helping the poor. As he became aware of conditions in factories, where poor people labored long hours for low wages, he encouraged them to strike. The strike failed, so Gandhi started a hunger strike. On the third day of the fast, the British raised the workers' wages by 35 percent.

In 1919 the British passed the Rowlatt Act, which allowed for secret trials and trials without appeals for people suspected of being "disloyal" to the government. When Gandhi's people staged a protest in Amritsar, officials opened fire on the unarmed protesters, killing 379 and wounding 1,200. This event, more than anything else, turned Gandhi against British rule. From then on, he didn't just protest unfair laws; he demanded Indian independence from Britain.

Behind Gandhi's nonviolent resistance was his belief in *satyagraha*, which literally means "truth force." His primary motivation was to draw attention to unfair practices or laws. He wanted to preserve a healing relationship with his opponents so that together they could correct the injustice, but first he had to make them recognize the injustice. Toward that end he employed several pressure tactics: strikes, boycotts, protests, and fasts.

In 1920, Gandhi called for massive "noncooperation" and the boycotting of British goods (especially cloth, which had made the British wealthy), schools, and jobs. Gandhi himself daily spun yarn for cloth so that he need not buy any British-made cloth. British officials repeatedly jailed Gandhi, and then released him in fear that he might die in prison, thus setting off more unrest.

One of Gandhi's most successful campaigns was his "march to the sea" to protest the salt tax in India. Gandhi attacked the tax as unjust and refused to buy the product. Instead, he took twenty-four days to march to the coast (at Dandi), where he scooped up natural salt from the sea. This was illegal, but women and children joined in his march, and the British realized they couldn't stop Gandhi and his followers. Days later they arrested 60,000 people, including many leaders in the Indian National Congress, for illegally collecting salt. Less than two weeks later, Gandhi himself was imprisoned.

Again and again, Gandhi (and his wife) was imprisoned and eventually released for promoting Indian independence. He believed that one day the British would rethink their position and grant India her independence. Toward that end, Gandhi continued to speak out and to fast whenever his demonstrations turned violent. Fasting was his way to stop the violence and to atone for the violent actions of his people.

Gandhi disrupted British rule through his strikes, his boycotts, and his noncooperation. Jailing him did nothing to decrease his incredible power. If anything, it enhanced it. Here was a man who sought only self-rule for his country. He had no desire for personal glory.

Gandhi valued India's relationship with Britain, and so did not resort to violence. He chose to work within the system. Because he always believed that justice would prevail, he succeeded in winning India's independence in 1947. Gandhi demonstrated his enormous strength, not through weapons and armies, but through his principled and relentless resistance.

Civil Rights and Martin Luther King, Jr.

Dr. Martin Luther King, Jr. was the son of a preacher who grew up to be a charismatic preacher himself. He used nonviolence to protest racial discrimination in the United States in the 1960s.

As Gandhi had done, King chose to work within the system. He encouraged resistance, but no violence, even though he and his protesters endured all kinds of violence themselves. Their faith in God (and their belief that justice would prevail) helped them through the harshest confrontations.

Racial discrimination was alive and well in the 1960s, especially in the Southern part of the United States. African-Americans were not allowed to use the same facilities as whites. They couldn't use the same bathrooms, water fountains, or entrances to buildings. They couldn't sit in the same sections on buses, and they couldn't be served in restaurants catering to whites only. Their schools were segregated and inferior to those for whites. In 1960 Cassius Clay won a gold medal for boxing in the Rome Olympics. He returned to his hometown in Kentucky, where he received a hero's welcome until he tried to get served in a whites-only restaurant. Clay, later known as Muhammad Ali, threw his gold medal into the Ohio River.

The distinction needs to be made here that the civil rights movement was *not a struggle against white people.* Just as Gandhi had protested injustice, so did the proponents of the civil rights movement. *This was a struggle against injustice.*

The Rosa Parks incident also was crucial to the civil rights movement. In 1956 local police arrested Rosa Parks for refusing to give up her seat on a bus to a white man. Her arrest led to a yearlong boycott of public transportation in Montgomery, Alabama. When blacks stopped using the buses, whites realized how much of their livelihood depended on the blacks. The only way that blacks would return to the buses was to abolish the segregated seating. Ultimately, whites had to bow to that pressure.

Sit-ins were another tactic used in the early 1960s. Blacks entered whites-only restaurants, sat down at the counters, and waited to be served. Whites were outraged at their audacity; police were baffled because the protesters were too quiet and courteous to justify using force

against them. This was when people first began to test
the strength of the protester's nonviolent convictions.
They pressed lighted cigarettes against the protesters, and
poured ketchup over their heads. When people tried
forcibly moving the protesters, they grabbed the counters
and hung on. The sit-ins led to beatings, harassment, and
mass arrests, but they succeeded in bringing discriminatory practices to the attention of the country. Newspapers
all over the United States carried pictures of protesters
sitting quietly in restaurants, waiting to be served, while
others tormented them.

King's use of freedom rides, in which blacks and whites
rode together in buses through parts of the South, was
meant to stir up controversy. Civil rights leaders wanted
to provoke a crisis to force government leaders to act in
their behalf. Knowing that the discriminatory practices
were morally (as well as legally) wrong, they stood by their
convictions and refused to meet violence with violence.

In 1961 police used fire hoses and tear gas on freedom
riders, and set police dogs on protesters, including children. Everything was captured on television; the people,
unaware of the degree of hostility toward integration,
watched it all.

Civil rights leaders held protests and demonstrations.
Even though the protesters did not intend violence, the
demonstrations often turned violent as outraged specta-
tors besieged them. It took enormous courage for them to
adhere to their principles and not given in to violence.
Their power lay in their resistance and capacity to endure
suffering.

Knowing how powerful the movement had become,
courts started to clamp down. In one city, the courts
issued a ban on all further demonstrations. King chose to
disregard the ban because it was unjust. As Gandhi had

done on many occasions, King also agreed to be jailed for breaking the law. He made it clear that he didn't agree with the law, but subscribed to a higher law "based on divine justice."

On August 28, 1963, more than a quarter million people of all races gathered near the Lincoln Memorial in Washington D.C. This was the largest single protest march in United States history, and it remained nonviolent. The peaceful march brought more recognition to the civil rights movement, and encouraged government leaders to support and end to racial discrimination.

With the success of the demonstrations and the increased media attention to the problems of discrimination, civil rights workers turned to voter registration drives. Blacks had been discouraged from registering to vote in the past; efforts in the 1960s to sign eligible blacks to vote prompted more white resistance (and acting out). Some whites attacked blacks waiting in line to register or arrested them on trumped-up charges.

But the nonviolent protesters prevailed over bigotry. The Civil Rights bill was signed into law on July 2, 1964. In 1965 President Lyndon Johnson signed the Voters Rights Act. In the meantime, Dr. Martin Luther King, Jr. received the 1963 Nobel Peace Prize.

USING NONVIOLENT TACTICS

Gandhi made an important point. We must continually search for the rightness of our position. As imperfect human beings, we can't claim to know the "absolute truth" in any given situation. Therefore, we should strive to work with our adversaries to find that truth. Our goal is not to believe in the inherent rightness of our position, but in truth itself.

Toward that end, you must be able to listen to your adversary and make every effort to understand his position. You must be able to convey your own feelings and needs to him so that both of you can work together to find a peaceful, suitable solution. These tactics are especially useful for teens, as you are expected to make more and more decisions for yourself.

HANDLING CONFLICT CREATIVELY

CHAPTER 3

Problem-Solving Skills*

n order to perform the skills required for complex
negotiating and mediating, you have to master the
basic problem-solving skills first.

RECOGNIZING YOUR FEELINGS

Naturally, before you can negotiate with another person,
you have to recognize how you're feeling first. That is not
always as easy as it sounds. Consider the emotion anger.
Most people think anger is a primary emotion, something
you feel directly after an experience. Actually, anger is a
secondary emotion; it arises after you've felt something
else first, usually hurt or fear. People who recognize they

---

*Ideas adapted from *Conflict Resolution: A Curriculum for Youth
Providers* (San Francisco, CA: The Community Board Program, Inc.
1990).

are angry don't often take the time to look at what they're feeling underneath the anger. That person might be embarrassed, fearful of losing something valuable (including her self-esteem), or hurt that she's already lost something or someone. It's much easier to deal with your anger when you can clarify what brought it on.

Some people have only a few words to describe their emotional states: happy, upset, and depressed. "Upset" and "depressed" cover everything including worried, sad, angry, tense, blue, tired, and scared. If you can't be specific about your feelings, you're not going to be able to convey them accurately to others, and that's one of the first steps in effective problem-solving.

Try to connect your feelings with the conflict at hand. Once you can recognize the connection between the event and the feeling, you will have a good idea what your needs are. If I'm feeling hurt because of something you did, I might need an apology. If I'm confused over something you said, I might need you to clarify what you meant. Feelings will clue you in to your needs.

And bear in mind that "needs" are not "positions." It is not helpful to adopt a particular position about what you want to have happen to remedy the conflict. If each side adopted an inflexible position, there never would be room to negotiate. Needs are what you have when you know what you require to feel better about a situation. "I need to feel respected and appreciated"; "I need to earn enough money to afford my car payment each month"; "I need some extra help with my algebra." Those are needs you might have. Positions assume there's only one way to meet your needs. "You have to give me a raise." "You have to give me more hours to work each month." "You have to give me a good grade in algebra."

DEVELOPING BETTER LISTENING SKILLS

No doubt you've experienced something like the following situation. You're looking through your closet for your favorite sweater, but it's nowhere in sight. You have a hunch it might be in your sister's closet, so you rummage through her closet. Sure enough, there it is, lying in a crumpled heap on the floor.

You're furious because you planned to wear it to the dance tonight. If your sister had just asked to borrow your sweater, you could have reminded her you needed it for tonight. You find her in the den watching television. "We need to talk," you say, holding up the wrinkled sweater.

"Oh, that," your sister says. "I wore it the other day skating. Don't worry, I'll wash it." She continues to watch television.

"Well, I wanted to wear it tonight. How's it going to get clean in half an hour?" you demand.

"Sorry," your sister says, looking at you briefly. "I know I should have asked you."

By now you're really fuming. She doesn't seem to be getting the picture.

"I'm really mad," you say, and then you stand in front of the TV set, blocking the picture.

"Okay, so you're mad," she says, looking up.

"Apparently you think you can just walk into my closet anytime," you start to say. You notice she has one eye on you and one eye on the TV.

"Are you even listening?" you say.

"I'm listening," your sister grumbles.

"No, you're not. You're still watching that game show."

"Well, I can do two things at once," she says, trying to peer around you.

"You never listen anyway. I'm going to start going through your closet and wearing what I please. . . ."

"Can you see what time it is? I'm supposed to call Tina back at 7:15. Is it 7:15 yet?" she asks.

In this example, neither person was demonstrating good listening or communication skills. Your first mistake was picking the wrong moment to take your sister to task. If you're going to talk over a problem with someone, make sure you pick a good moment for both of you, not simply when you feel the need to say something.

Your sister, though, wasn't really listening, and thought that half her attention was enough. It isn't. People want you to make eye contact with them; they don't want to compete with the TV or any other activity. Your sister only made brief, unconvincing eye contact. Furthermore, she interrupted you while you were talking, bringing up something entirely unrelated to the subject at hand.

The most important skill you can develop is your ability to listen well. But listening is not a passive activity. It's actually hard work. Most people don't listen effectively. While the other party is talking, instead of listening, they are thinking up their rebuttal.

To teach my students how to listen, I give them the task of listening to someone with whom they strongly disagree. To show that they've listened (without putting their own two cents in), I ask them to write down the other person's main points. I do not want them to add their counterpoints; I want them to concentrate so entirely on this other person's point of view that they are able to reconstruct the conversation and the way the person seemed to be feeling.

This task is obviously very difficult. Try it yourself. Concentrating on someone else's view without thinking up your rebuttals in the meantime is hard. Few people can do it the first time they try.

When you listen to someone, you face him and make direct eye contact. In American culture, not making eye contact suggests you're lying, not interested in what's happening, or feeling guilty about something. Of course, that's not always true, but you should avoid stances that will create misunderstandings.

ACTIVE LISTENING

The point of good listening is to develop empathy, the ability to see another person's situation through his eyes, not yours. This is an active process that requires concentration.

First, in order to understand what he thinks, you have to get him to talk. You can't assume you know what he means all the time, either, so you may need to ask him to clarify his points.

You can reflect on how he's nonverbally communicating as well. Maybe he's not aware he looks angry when he's talking to you. When you say, "It seems as if you're angry about this because you're raising your voice and you've got your arms crossed." This technique is called "reflecting." You reflect back what you see happening along with what you hear the other person saying. Paraphrasing the content of their talk is "restating" but incorporating how you perceive them as they talk is "reflecting." After a long discussion, it's important to summarize what you've heard because what you think you've heard may not be the same as what was actually said. Finally, it's important to show the other person you appreciate their taking the time to explain things to you. This is called "validating the person." When two people are at odds on an issue, it's especially important that they validate each other even when they can't agree on the issue at stake. Here's a quick rundown on the six active listening techniques:

Skill	Sample questions
Encourage	"Tell me more about that" "What else happened?"
Clarify	"And what does that mean?" "So, how did you feel then?"
Restate	"What you're saying is . . ." "So, you think . . ."
Reflect	"You looked a little anxious when you said that." "You seem sad about that."
Summarize	"You're upset with me because . . ." "You'd like us to spend more time together."
Validate	"Thanks for telling me how you feel about that." "I'm glad you felt you could tell me that."

If you practice these six skills, you'll find yourself concentrating more on the person talking than on what you're thinking. The other person will feel respected because he was actually listened to. Sometimes, that's all that's needed to end a conflict.

DEVELOPING YOUR COMMUNICATION SKILLS

In order to keep someone talking so that you finally understand his point of view, you must be careful not to interrupt or turn off the conversation.

How many of you actually want to pursue a conversation with someone when she says, "How could you do something so stupid?" or "You know, if I were you, I would have done that all different."

Lecturing people, threatening them, analyzing them, or judging them puts a stop to most conversations. People get defensive and clam up. When you communicate with others, be very careful that you won't be perceived as preacher, teacher, judge and jury.

Sending "I" Messages

When something bothers you, it's best to speak to the person in a direct way. Instead of launching an attack (which only makes people defensive), tell him *specifically what is bothering you, how it makes you feel*, and *what the consequences are to you*.

For example, you might tell someone, "When I see you spit gum on the lawn, I get angry because I figure someone will step on it and track it in the house. Then, I'll have to clean it out of the carpet."

It is important to convey the first three parts: the behavior I perceive to be the problem, how it makes me feel and the consequences for me. Usually, the other person will step in at this point and offer a solution. But if that doesn't happen, there is a last part—*and what I want you to do is. . . .* —which conveys how you'd like the other person to correct the situation. This can be very effective, but I have found that more often, people prefer to think up their own solution to the problem.

Giving "I" messages makes your point concisely without attacking the other person.

Styles of Behavior

You convey your style of behavior by the way you speak to others, the words you use, and your body language. People fall into three categories: aggressive, assertive, and submissive (also called nonassertive or passive). I prefer to call it submissive because that word better captures the behavior of the person.

If a person is aggressive, he will speak loudly, perhaps glare at his opponent, shake his fist, threaten with words or gestures, and move in too closely. The aggressive person makes others feel uncomfortable because he freely violates their space.

If a person is submissive, he will speak quietly or mumble (because he's not sure of himself); he'll keep his eyes on the floor and will stand away from his opponent. He'll also be quick to apologize even when things are not his fault, and he won't stand up for his rights. He may make others feel uncomfortable, because he is easily taken advantage of.

If a person is assertive, he will bring up problems with people, looking them directly in the eye, but not intimidating them. He speaks clearly without screaming, and he does not infringe on their territory. The assertive person is just as concerned with his own rights as he is with the other person's.

Assertiveness is a skill you can learn. Many schools offer assertiveness training workshops, as it is a skill that can be developed in a relatively short period of time.

Consider the following situation, and think what your response might be.

Mrs. Jameson and her teenage son lived next door to Mr. and Mrs. Thompson. Twice a week, both families put their trash out for the garbage men to pick up. However, Mr. Thompson never put a cover on his trash. By the time the garbage men got to his street, Mr. Thompson's garbage had blown all over Mrs. Jameson's yard. Mrs. Jameson's son had to pick up the trash because he was the first person home.

If you were Mrs. Jameson's son, how would you handle the problem?

The aggressive response: Mrs. Jameson's son scoops up all the trash, carts it over to the Thompsons' front door, rings their bell, and then proceeds to dump the trash on the front steps. When Mrs. Thompson answers the door, the boy yells, "I believe this is your trash. If you can't find a cover for your garbage, you're going to find this piled up on your front steps every week." He storms off, trailing trash.

The submissive (or passive response): Mrs. Jameson's son cleans up the trash without complaining. When Mr. Thompson drives up and spots him, Mr. Thompson hollers, "Oops, sorry about that." Mrs. Jameson's son only smiles and says, "It's okay; I didn't mind picking it up." Mr. Thompson waves his hand and goes inside. Mrs. Jameson's son feels furious and has a headache.

The passive-aggressive response (which is a combination of the aggressive and submissive): Mrs. Jameson's son picks up all the garbage and then leaves his neighbor's trash can by their side door so that when the trash blows, it'll end up all over their lawn. He doesn't say a word to his neighbors.

The assertive response: Mrs. Jameson's son picks up the trash and stores it in his garbage can, which has a cover.

Then he goes over to talk with Mrs. Thompson. When she comes to the door, the boy tells her that their trash has been blowing all over his yard because there's no cover on the can. He recognizes that they have been good neighbors through the years and wonders if she'd work with him on a solution to the problem. Note that the boy presents it as a mutual problem, not his neighbors' problem. He remains open to discussion.

What would be the likely reaction to the aggressive response? Escalation? No doubt, Mr. Thompson would have been angry at this teenager's behavior, and might have done something similar himself. The feud would only have continued.

What would have been the reaction to the submissive response? Probably nothing. Since the boy hadn't made any issue out of it, the neighbors didn't have to do anything.

What would have been the reaction to the passive-aggressive response? Confusion. The Thompsons would have felt angry that the garbage was now all over their lawn, but they wouldn't know for sure that the teenager planned it that way. So, the conflict would continue, and neither side would be the wiser.

What if Mrs. Thompson had said to the assertive teenager, "I see that we need a cover, but you know, we had one, and the garbage men must have lost it for us. One day, it just wasn't there anymore. I probably should have mentioned this, but I figured I'd leave well enough alone. It's your dogs that keep getting into our trash now and strew it all over your yard."

Mrs. Jameson's son looks surprised. He hadn't realized his own dogs were at fault.

"Well, I'll make sure we keep the back gate locked so our dogs won't get into your trash," he offered.

Seeing that the teenager was trying to be helpful, Mrs. Thompson smiled and said, "And I'll send Mr. Thompson out tonight to buy another lid for the can. I'm sure it's not fun when the trash flies all over your lawn."

Because the neighbors had listened to each other, the conflict was easily resolved. Both contributed to the solution. That wouldn't have been possible if the teenager hadn't brought up the problem in the first place, or had behaved aggressively. Aggressive behavior, even the passive-aggressive kind, keeps a conflict simmering. However, passive behavior doesn't specify what the problem is.

Jessie is a nonassertive teenager. Whenever she's mad about something, she makes a big production out of walking out of the room. If her mother doesn't pick up on the fact that Jessie is upset, Jessie turns her stereo up loud.

Jessie's mom knocks on her door. "Jessie, turn down the music!"

Jessie turns it down a hair, all the time thinking, "Come on, Mom. Ask me why I'm mad."

If her mom still doesn't figure it out, Jessie starts storming around her room, slamming drawers. The noise is bound to bring her mom running.

Finally, her mom knocks again. "What is your problem?" she asks.

"Nothing," Jessie says, thinking, "Okay, Mom. Just ask me once more, and I'll tell you."

"Jessie, something's bothering you. Do you want to talk about it?"

"Oh, all right," Jessie says, reluctantly opening the door while thinking, "Finally you ask!"

If you don't bring the conflict up, you can't expect others to figure it out from your behavior.

Providing Good Feedback

To clarify the conflict for the other person so that the two of you can work to resolve it, you have to provide the person with good feedback.

Tell him specifically what is wrong. Simply describe what happened that bothered you; don't add judgmental comments. Judgmental remarks only make a person defensive. When someone is on the defensive he feels like he's being attacked, and he's not going to listen to you.

Give your feedback in a timely manner. If you're mad at your best friend for not calling you when she promised, don't wait a week to tell her about it. When you feed your anger for a week or more, you end up clobbering the other person with all of your stored-up anger, instead of being able to explain specifically what set you off.

Even though you try to give your feedback in a timely manner, be sensitive to occasions when the other person might not be receptive to hearing this feedback. For example, if your mother comes home from work upset because her boss chewed her out about an assignment, it's probably not a good time to bring up a conflict with her. As long as you don't let the conflict drag on for days, you can choose the best time to bring it up.

USING YOUR SKILLS TO PROBLEM-SOLVE

Once you've developed your listening skills and learned to communicate assertively, you've ready to combine these skills to problem-solve your way through a conflict. We'll examine specific conflict situations in the next chapter; in this section, I'll give you the general rules.

Identify the Problem

When faced with a conflict, do your homework first. Figure out what is specifically bothering you, and how it's making you feel. Consider how you'd like the situation to be resolved. Then seek out the person with whom you are having the conflict, and ask if he'd be willing to sit down with you and talk about the problem. It's important to find a time that's mutually convenient. If either of you is pressed for time or in a bad mood, you'll want to rush through the proceedings, and that won't be helpful.

You'll want to work with the other person to solve the conflict, but it always helps to have some kind of solution in mind from the outset. It's not helpful if your partner says, "Well, what do you think we should do about this?" and you reply, "I have no idea." That makes it sound as if you were expecting him to solve the problem himself.

Some people think the conflict is settled once they've brought it up and shared their concerns. But, unless the two sides can come up with a solution, the conflict is merely identified, not resolved.

Communicate and Listen to the Other Side

While you should have some idea of what it would take to solve this conflict, be willing to consider all options. The "winner" isn't the person who comes up with the best solution. A good solution should make you both winners.

Keep an open mind. If you practice reflective listening, you may see a different side to the problem. Then you may see where your original solution wouldn't work. The key to finding good solutions is to be flexible.

Be fair. In talking your situation over with the other person, you may discover that you're to blame for part of the conflict. Accept your part of the blame, and apologize. Too many people think an apology is an admission of weakness; it isn't. It's usually harder to apologize for something than it is to deny responsibility. If you want to settle things fairly, you have to own your part in any conflict. Apologies go a long way toward rectifying wrong.

Brainstorm Solutions

Here's the fun part of conflict resolution. Before you settle on a quick fix, spend some time tossing around some possible solutions. Think of anything, even if the ideas are too impractical to count. Often, good ideas have sprung from a seemingly impractical one. You want to generate as many solutions as possible so that one will surface that could satisfy both parties' needs.

For example, imagine that you're recovering from a bad illness. You've missed a month or more of classes, and you need to negotiate with your teacher how to catch up with your homework. You start to brainstorm options.

You volunteer, "You could cut down on the amount of work."

The teacher says, "Our families could take a vacation together while you and I caught up on schoolwork."

"I could stay late each day to get caught up on assignments."

"Your sister could tutor you, since she took my class last year. Then you could test out of some of the material."

"Or I could take an incomplete this semester, and work through the summer to make it up."

You get the picture. Some of the ideas are, of course, more practical than others; the point, though, is to keep coming up with ideas (no matter how crazy) until they've run out.

Once you've run out of ideas, take a closer look at them. Discard the ridiculous ones, and see if you can combine others to come up with an even better solution. Narrow down your choices.

Summarize Contributions to Solution

Once you've come to an agreement, summarize what you'll both do to resolve the conflict. Some people talk over so many options, they forget which option they agreed to. Or they forget what their contribution was supposed to be. The conflict is rarely resolved through talk alone; it's the actions you take that resolve it.

STAYING NEUTRAL

If conflict resolution always ran smoothly, more people would want to engage in it. Unfortunately, what often happens is that as emotions increase during a conflict, judgment decreases. If you find yourself in the midst of a conflict and people's tempers are flaring, suggest a break so you both can cool down. If you're the one who is calm, ask the other person to tell you what he's feeling and why. Giving an angry person time to vent, and listening attentively so that you can understand why he feels the way he does, often defuses the anger. Sometimes, all a person needs is another person to hear him out, and he can regain his composure. Only continue problem-solving when the emotions have died down.

THOUGHTS ON POWER

Don't assume the person with the authority is the one with all the power. Remember the power of nonviolent resistance. Calm persistence can offset anyone's authority. The person with power is usually the one who believes he is powerful.

CHAPTER ◇ 4

Putting Your Skills
to Work

Different situations call on you to use different skills. Collaborating with your partner—and it helps to think of the other person in the conflict as a partner, not an adversary—is preferable because both sides can get the majority of their needs met. But, in the end, you have to be able to recognize when it is time to collaborate, and when it's better to withdraw. Consider the following scenarios.

CONFLICT IN A RELATIONSHIP

Paula and Erin were best friends in high school. In their senior year another girl, Amanda, moved into Paula's neighborhood. Soon the three of them were doing everything together, but since Paula and Amanda lived near each other, gradually they started doing more things together than Paula and Erin did.

Erin watched the growing relationship between Paula and Amanda. At first she was angry with Paula for changing the way things had been, but she didn't think it was right to be angry. So she grew distant, spending more time with her family.

Paula and Amanda became a twosome, excluding Erin from more and more activities. After a while, Paula seemed to forget she'd ever been best friends with Erin.

One day, Erin decided to talk with Paula about all of this. She recognized that she was feeling angry, but more than that, she realized that she was sad at being left out by her friends. That's the first step in addressing a conflict: clarifying your feelings.

Erin met Paula at her locker later that day and asked if they could meet after school "to talk about something that was bothering her." Paula said, "Sure, how about going to the diner for french fries?"

Erin agreed. Later, when they squeezed into a booth, Erin began, "Paula, I know you and Amanda have become good friends, but I'm feeling really left out these days. Things don't seem the same between us anymore."

Paula looked puzzled. "Well, you're welcome to come along with us. You just always have other things to do."

"That's because you don't have time for me," Erin said.

"That's not true," Paula said.

"Wait a minute," Erin broke in. "I didn't want this to turn into an argument. I wanted to tell you I miss our being close friends. When you walk home with Amanda now, I feel left out. You haven't returned the last three calls I've made to you."

Here, Erin is confronting Paula in an assertive manner instead of waiting for Paula to figure out what's wrong. She gives Paula specific feedback about what's bothering her without being judgmental about it. Then she waits to hear what Paula has to say.

Paula tried to say things weren't that much different, then she stopped mid-sentence. "I guess things are a little different," she said. "But let me tell you why. Amanda's father has emphysema and will probably die. You remember when my dad died three years ago? Well, I kind of understand what Amanda is going through, and I feel close to her. It's not that we don't have room for you; it's just that Amanda and I have something extra in common."

Erin saw the situation in a different light. "You're saying you've been spending more time with Amanda because you have something important in common and you feel close to her."

Here, she practices reflective listening. She tries to see things through Paula's eyes and then restates what she's heard to Paula.

"That's right," Paula said. "It has nothing to do with you. It's more to do with us right now."

"I see. So, it's not that you two didn't like my company?" Here Erin is asking for further clarification.

"No, did it seem that way to you? I guess I wasn't very sensitive to your needs while I was trying to be so sensitive to Amanda's. You're still my good friend, too. What do you think we should do?"

"Well, I guess I jumped to my own conclusions a little too fast," Erin said. "I just thought you guys didn't like me or something. I hoped we could get back to doing things together more."

"Sure we can. Why don't the three of us go roller skating this Friday night?"

"Sounds good to me," Erin said. "I understand why you two got along so fast; I'll try to remember that in the future and not jump to so many conclusions." Here she summarizes what she can do to help improve the situation.

This may sound like a lot of work: clarifying (first to yourself, then to others), listening, and communicating your needs assertively. Actually, you'll discover that it only takes a lot of time in the beginning. Once you've learned the steps and are willing to face conflicts as soon as they come up, you'll find that the conflicts become less and less frequent. What really takes time is trying to remedy what got out of control because no one was willing to address it in the first place.

DEALING WITH DIFFICULT PEOPLE

It's hard to remain assertive with difficult people because one's natural tendency is to withdraw or fight back. However, calmly restating one's expectations usually pays off in the end. The situation is more complicated when you're dealing with a difficult person with whom you have a lasting relationship.

Tara had a love/hate relationship with her Aunt DaLana, who seemed to have a knack for pointing out Tara's every flaw. Whenever Tara visited this aunt, she ended up feeling defensive and beleaguered. Since her mother's sister was always going to be in the family, Tara decided to bring the conflict out in the open. She decided she was going to tell her aunt the very next time the aunt offended her.

One Saturday, Aunt DaLana stopped by to go shopping with Tara's mother. While Tara's mom finished getting dressed, Tara offered her aunt some leftover cinnamon rolls and a cup of coffee. Tara sat down at the table.

"These are good cinnamon rolls," her aunt said.

"I thought so, too," Tara said.

"You probably shouldn't eat them too often, though," her aunt said. "They probably are very fattening."

"We don't have them often," Tara assured her.

Aunt DaLana peered over her glasses at Tara. "I shouldn't hope so. Looks like you've put on some weight since I last saw you."

Tara felt her face reddening. "I don't think so," she mumbled.

"Well, cinnamon rolls will do it every time. You better start thinking about your weight, you know. When you get this age, those pounds have a way of hanging around." She peered at Tara again. "You've got some pimples around your chin. You really ought to wash better."

Tara was starting to feel exasperated. Why did she have to listen to this?

"Aunt DaLana," Tara began hesitantly. "I feel embarrassed when you mention my weight and complexion."

"Oh, you needn't be embarrassed. I'm family, you know."

"Yes," Tara agreed, "but it hurts my feelings when you point these things out."

"Don't be so thin-skinned," her aunt said.

"Well, I would just appreciate it if you wouldn't bring the subject up."

Aunt DaLana scowled. She looked around the room. "Go see if your mom is ready to go," she said. She pushed herself away from the table.

Tara felt rebuffed. "I'll see," she said.

Her aunt sat back with her arms crossed and her lips pursed. Tara knew she was mad, but she figured the more she said, the worse things would get. She got up and went looking for her mother. "It doesn't do any good to be assertive with her," she thought.

Sometimes, you have to continue being assertive with difficult people until they change their behavior. Other times, it may not feel worth the effort. For those occasions, you may want to use the technique called "clouding." It's a handy little device for changing the subject when the subject isn't one you're enjoying.

Clouding is asking a question that is so off the wall that it catches the other person off guard. She gets sidetracked without at first knowing what hit her. The question has to be bizarre and confusing, so that the other person is left wondering if she's been had. However, it will succeed in derailing the subject under discussion. Clouding is a technique for avoiding a bigger conflict when you can't break off the relationship.

For example, Tara might have used clouding on her aunt.

"Looks like you've put on weight since I last saw you," Aunt DaLana says.

Tara ignores this comment and asks instead, "Aunt DaLana, if the earth is always spinning on its axis, why do you suppose it never just spins right out of orbit and out of our universe?" She looks at her aunt intently.

Her aunt looks perplexed. "What was that?" she asked.

"You know, I was thinking about the earth spinning and rotating, and well, I wondered how come it never just spins right out of the galaxy?"

Her aunt continues to look suspicious. "I don't know," she says finally.

"Okay," Tara says. "I'll go see if Mom is ready to go yet."

Clouding is a diversionary tactic; it doesn't replace honest assertive communication. However, it can take the focus off an unpleasant subject.

The next time a salesclerk makes some rude comment to you, instead of cringing (or telling her off), throw out a clouding question. "Have you ever thought about which way trees grow? I mean, do they grow down as well as up and out the branches, and could you really measure the growth of the roots without killing the tree?" Of course, you haven't asserted yourself, but you will end the discussion. And you can smile to yourself as you walk away, leaving the clerk wondering if you were really asking her about trees or making a joke.

DEALING WITH AN UNHAPPY CUSTOMER

The skills I describe in this example can apply to any situation where you're dealing with someone who's complaining. While it's best to lend an ear to someone who's upset and wanting to vent, there is a technique you can use to lower the intensity of a situation. It's called fogging. A fogging response is one where you find some grain of truth in what the other person is saying, and you agree with him or her. For most people, it calms a situation down. You might say, "That's probably true" or "You might be right" or "Maybe so." Leave it at that; when you include, "but . . .", you're implying "but here's where you're wrong." Simply agree, and leave it at that.

Roger worked weekends at a bookstore in the mall. He occasionally had to deal with disgruntled customers. One afternoon, a woman came to his register to return the latest best-seller.

"I got this book for my birthday," she said. "But I already read it at the library. I'd like to return it."

"Certainly," Roger said. "Do you have your receipt?"

"Of course, I don't have a receipt," the woman said. "It was a gift."

"Well, if you don't have a receipt, I'll have to issue you a voucher for another book of equal value here. I'm sure you can find something else."

The woman frowned. "You don't understand," she said. "I don't want anything else. I want a refund."

Roger felt his stomach flip-flop. "I'm sorry; it's company policy that we issue vouchers when the customer doesn't have a receipt."

"Well, I never heard of that before," she said.

Roger pointed out the sign bearing the strict policy. "It's always been there," he said.

The woman nodded. "First time anyone has ever mentioned it," she said. "Look, I come here a lot. I'm a good customer. Can't you just give me a cash refund this time? I wanted to get something else with this money."

Roger's face started to redden. "I can't do that," he said.

"Well, that's an unfair policy," the woman fumed. She was raising her voice, and other customers were glancing over at her. Roger's boss had told him to keep customers from making scenes. It drove other customers away.

Roger remembered the fogging technique he'd learned in class. "You're right," he said. "It does seem unfair in this case."

The woman looked at him. "You mean you'll give me the refund?"

"No," Roger said, keeping eye contact with the woman. "But I agree with you that it seems unfair. I'm sure you had thought you could spend this money on something else."

"I'd wanted to buy some makeup," the woman confided. "You can't get that in a bookstore," she said.

"You're right about that," Roger said.

The woman sighed and then said, "Well, I suppose the makeup will have to come out of next week's paycheck. I'll take the voucher."

Gayle was backing her dad's car out of the school parking lot unfortunately at the exact same time another student was backing her car out. The two cars collided. Gayle got out and looked at the bumper on her dad's car. It was scratched and dented. The other car appeared fine.

Gayle felt a lump in her throat. "My dad's going to kill me when he sees this," she said to the other driver.

"Well, my car's okay. I wouldn't report it if I were you."

"Well, I'll have to tell my dad," she said.

All the way home she worried about how she was going to tell her dad. He would just go ballistic. She'd never hear the end of it.

When Mr. Olmstead got home, Gayle immediately told him about the accident.

"Weren't you watching where you were going?" her dad asked. "Let me see the bumper."

He checked the car for further damage she might have missed. "Probably knocked the alignment out, too," he said.

"I'm really sorry," Gayle said. She waited for him to start haranguing her.

"Well, sorry doesn't do much for the bumper. I can't believe you were so careless," he said.

"I agree, it was pretty careless," Gayle said.

"Here I trust you to take the car to school and you can't even back out of the parking lot without running into someone. I'm just furious."

"You've got every right to be angry. It was careless of me."

"It *was* careless of you," her dad agreed.

"Is it going to be expensive to fix?" she asked.

"Of course, it's going to be expensive to fix. And if I report it to the insurance company, your rate will go through the roof!"

"You're probably right. They'd raise my insurance rates. I really feel bad about this, Dad."

"Well, I guess you've probably learned a lesson," he said. Never assume you're the only one backing out of a parking space. Always look over your shoulder."

"I intend to be more careful," Gayle said.

"Well, you weren't hurt, were you?" her dad asked, looking at her now instead of the car.

"No, we weren't going very fast at all."

"Well, that's good," he said. "We can always fix a car."

DEALING WITH PASSIVE-AGGRESSIVENESS

When someone is passive-agressive, he or she does not get openly angry, and does not directly communicate his or her true feelings. Instead, the feelings surface in an indirect, or even unconscious, way. Thus, when dealing with a passive-aggressive person, you can best address the conflict by bringing it out in the open.

For examples, imagine that your boyfriend promised to take you shopping Saturday afternoon. You had the feeling he didn't really want to take you, that he only agreed because he couldn't think of a reason not to. By 3:00, he hasn't shown up, and you're fuming. This is the third time he has stood you up. Why does it seem he always forgets the times you want to go do something? He's always prompt when you're going to the hockey games.

You decide to call him at 3:30. He answers the phone on the first ring.

"Darren, why are you home?" you say. "You said you were going to take me to the mall this afternoon."

"I'm so sorry," he exclaims. "I forgot all about it."

"This is the third time you've forgotten," you say.

"Well, it wasn't like I did it on purpose," he says.

"I'm beginning to wonder," you say.

"Oh, come on. We can go tomorrow."

"What I want to know is why you just don't say you'd rather not take me shopping. I could deal with that better than your forgetfulness."

"It was a mistake," he says.

"Maybe," you say. "But it feels more like you just don't want to do this, and that's okay because I've got other friends to go shopping with. I could go with Catherine."

"Really? I bet you'd have more fun shopping with a girlfriend. I'd be kind of a drag," he says.

"Look, just be upfront with me from now on. If you don't want to do something, say so. I'm not going to crumble," you say.

"Then you'll still go to the hockey game tonight?"

Another common passive-aggressive behavior is *not* communicating your needs, but implicitly asking for someone's help or favor. Someone could make an open-ended statement such as "I don't know how I'm going to be able to paint my bedroom when the ladder is broken . . ." and quietly wait for you to offer your ladder—and your time—to help. This can be extremely uncomfortable when you don't want to do what the person is asking. In cases like this, you can bring the question out in the open by saying "Were you hoping I could volunteer my ladder?" and reminding the person that it is okay to ask you upfront. Then, decide if volunteering the ladder is something that you *really* can or can't do, and explain your reasons why.

This type of passive-aggressive behavior may seem manipulative and designed to make you fee guilty, but it more likely arises out of someone's own insecurities and fear of being open. If you handle it in a friendly and assertive way, you can show that communication is the best way to solve problems.

NEGOTIATING ON THE JOB

What kinds of conflicts require negotiating, which is a more formal process of problem-solving? Most people think negotiations have to do with money. People who haggle over how much to pay for something at a garage sale are negotiating. People who request a certain salary before starting a new job are negotiating. People who want a markdown on department store merchandise are negotiating.

But there are other things to negotiate besides how much you're going to pay for something. You might need to negotiate your work schedule (what days or hours you'll work); you might need to negotiate your benefits (not all employees get the same package); you might need to negotiate job responsibilities.

Sometimes you may need to negotiate when to take a makeup exam for a teacher. You may need to negotiate leaving class early or getting another hall pass.

Some people even negotiate for a living. They negotiate contracts for companies, sell products and negotiate service agreements on those products. Some act as negotiators in other people's disputes (which makes them mediators or arbitrators, depending on their authority to resolve the disputes).

What negotiators have in common is a desire to get their needs met, or the needs of those they represent. All of us need to negotiate in our lives. Parents negotiate with their kids to get more cooperation around the home; husbands negotiate with their wives (and vice versa) when they have differences of opinion; teachers and students negotiate, as do landlords and tenants.

Steps in Negotiating

Distinguish between what you want and what you need to gain from this negotiation. Our "wants" are things we might like to have but we can get along without. Our "needs" are more important.

In discussing a benefit package with my potential employer, I may *want* three weeks paid vacation, a company car to use, and season tickets for the Bulls. What I *need*, though, is the vacation and medical/dental insurance coverage.

If you present all your "wants" as "needs," you're going to overwhelm your partner. She won't see a way to meet all of your needs and hers as well. If she finds out that some of your needs are really wants, she may expect you to mix up needs and wants in the future too, and therefore won't take your genuine needs as seriously. So distinquishing between wants and needs saves you time and credibility in the long run.

Paul has been working only a few months for Mr. Ramirez. He needs to start saving for the senior prom, but at his current earnings, he still won't have enough money saved to rent a tux, buy flowers and dinner, and make his car payments. He decides he needs a raise.

Mr. Ramirez is reluctant to give Paul a raise. Paul hasn't even worked for him a year, and although he has no complaints about Paul's work, he doesn't want to give him a raise just yet.

If the two of them adopted inflexible positions (and positions are usually inflexible), neither would get anywhere. Paul's position would be: "Give me a raise." Mr. Ramirez's position would be: "I'm not giving you a raise."

But instead of focusing on their positions (what they wanted to happen), they talked about their needs. Paul confessed that what he needed was more money because he was trying to save to pay off his car before college and take his girlfriend to the senior prom. Mr. Ramirez acknowledged that he had the money to give Paul a raise, but he wanted Paul to earn the money, not receive it simply because he'd been there three months.

Knowing their needs, Mr. Ramirez offered, "But I'd be willing to give you more hours to work here. You've been working halftime. I'd be willing to increase your time to as much as you wanted."

Paul thought for a minute. He could handle the extra work, and it beat finding a second part-time job. So he agreed. Mr. Ramirez gave him additional responsibilities for which he paid extra. The arrangement satisfied both their needs: Paul got more money (just not in the form of a raise for the same amount of work), and Mr. Ramirez didn't have to give away something for nothing (as he envisioned a premature raise). If both had stuck to their original position (their wants), no solution would have presented itself. Even a compromise (Mr. Ramirez gives Paul half of the raise he requests) wouldn't have met either person's needs.

Not everyone can decipher his partner's needs (and remember: conflicts stem from different psychological needs) ahead of time. If you're not sure, ask your partner during the early stages of negotiating what his needs are. If he says, "I will only pay you $6 an hour," try to rephrase your question so that you get at his "needs," not his "position." Does he need to save the company money? Does he need to keep all his new employees in the same earnings bracket?

In trying to figure out your partner's needs, ask open-ended questions that ask for more than a yes, or no, or other simple answer. You need for him to tell you how he's feeling, so ask questions that begin with, "How do you feel about . . ." or "Why do you like . . ." instead of "Do you like . . ." and "How much are you willing to consider?"

Not all negotiators want to negotiate (or at least to negotiate fairly). You need to set the ground rules early. So when you need to negotiate a conflict, ask the other person when is a good time for the two of you to sit down and work on a solution. Then, ask if he's willing to seek a solution that will meet both of your needs. Even if he

PUTTING YOUR SKILLS TO WORK ◇ 59

intends to hang tough on his position, he must agree to seek a solution satisfactory to both of you.

Dealing with Hardball Tactics

When you value the relationship with your negotiating partner, you must treat him with respect. You don't break promises with people you care about, and you don't play dirty. Therefore, you won't bully or play dirty with your negotiating partner. Manipulating others may not seem as destructive as out and out aggression, but it's still dishonest. If you want to preserve a good relationship with your partner, you've got to be fair.

However, you should be prepared to deal with people who seem to be locked into their positions.

Aggression. If your negotiating partner starts raising his voice, leaning in close to your face, or adopting a threatening posture, he is being aggressive. Sit back, be quiet for a while (to calm yourself as well as tone down the situation), and ignore the threats. If it's hard for you to relax around such hostility, try to imagine your negotiating partner in a less flattering light. Think of him or her naked, or wearing clothes backward. Whatever brings a smile to your face, think of that, and you'll be less intimidated. Then, attempt to defuse the situation by speaking calmly yourself and taking care not to adopt a "defensive" aggressive stance.

If the intimidation continues, bluntly ask your partner if he's trying to intimidate you. Chances are, when you point out his tactics and refuse to let them intimidate you, he'll drop the aggressive stance. If he doesn't, simply suggest continuing the negotiation at a time when emotions are not running so high.

Changing the Subject and Interrupting. If a negotiator gets off the topic under discussion, remind him of it. Mention that the other issue is not on the agenda, and that you're not ready to deal with anything else right now.

Likewise, a person who interrupts is trying to throw you off balance. Remind your partner that he's interrupting, and continue to talk. If he continues to interrupt, suggest taking a break.

Uncomfortable Surroundings. Some negotiators will give you the hard, uncomfortable chair, or have you sit where the sun shines in your eyes. This tactic is meant to make you feel uncomfortable and unsure about how to remedy the situation. If you find yourself in uncomfortable surroundings, bring your discomfort out in the open. Ask for a different chair; ask to move to another spot so that the sun isn't in your eyes; if the room is uncomfortably cold, ask to turn down the air conditioner. If you're straightforward with someone, he or she will usually give up the unfair tactic.

The Good Guy/Bad Guy Routine. Some people try to get you on their side with this technique when you are negotiating with two people at once. One person threatens you and acts belligerent; the other guy pretends not to like this person's behavior and tries to get you to warm up to him. If the tactic works, you end up allying yourself with this actual adversary (probably conceding a lot of your needs for the negotiation). If this happens to you, bring it into the open. Simply ask the two people you're negotiating with if they're using the "good guy/bad guy routine." Mentioning the tactic in apparent innocence is usually enough to get them to drop it.

When the Negotiation Is Stuck

Suggest a break if you're tired and the negotiation is stuck. Sometimes, perspective returns once you're rested. Watch your tone of voice and other nonverbal signals. If you start raising your voice, you may be intimidating your partner. Never point your finger in someone's face, no matter how mad you are. That's an inflammatory gesture, designed to antagonize. Likewise, don't stare at your feet, or wring your hands when asking for something (which are submissive gestures). Your partner is not likely to take your needs seriously if you act so conciliatory.

And most important, always look your partner in the eyes. People who can't bring themselves to look in your eyes appear deceitful. Maybe they're only shy, but inevitably others view people with downcast eyes as untrustworthy.

The rest of the steps in a negotiation are exactly the same as when you problem-solve.

- State your needs clearly, then use reflective listening.
- Once you've clarified your needs and your partner's needs, brainstorm solutions together.
- When you've agreed on a solution, decide how you'll implement it.
- Follow up on the details.

Let's look at two girls negotiating on the job.

Fran and Debra both work at a department store. Debra wanted to take some days off at Christmas so she could go back East to visit her parents. When she asked her manager for the time off, the manager said Fran had already requested a Christmas vacation and the store couldn't afford to let two people off at that time of year. Debra decided to negotiate with her friend for the days. She asked Fran to stop by after her shift because she wanted to work something out with her. Fran met her in the break room at five.

Debra sat down with her and told her about their requests for the same days off at Christmas. She was hoping Fran would offer to give her the days, but she knew that wasn't likely.

Fran didn't say anything, so Debra said, "Look, I'd like to negotiate with you. I'm not asking you to give in to me; I want both of us to be happy with the arrangement. After all, you're my friend."

"But it sounds like we both want the same thing. One of us isn't going to get what she wants," Fran said.

"So far, it looks like we both want the same thing, but maybe we don't have the same needs. What I want is a Christmas vacation. What I need is to spend some time with my parents."

Fran thought for a minute. "What I want is a Christmas vacation too. What I need is Christmas Eve off, Christmas day, and the day after, because my boyfriend's parents will be in town then."

"Well, we could both stage a strike and then we wouldn't have to worry about our vacations," Debra said.

"Or one of us could bribe management into granting both our requests."

"Seriously, you know I'd probably have better luck booking a flight home right after Christmas than I would right before," Debra said. "If you agreed to move your vacation up a couple of days so that you still had Christmas Eve, Christmas day and the day after, I could take my vacation a little later and still have the New Year's holidays."

"I guess I could switch things around, as long as I'm still keeping those days," Fran said. "It means a lot to my boyfriend to spend time with his parents, you know." She thought a minute. "Sure, I can agree to that."

"Great, then," Debra said. "I'll put in my request and remind you tomorrow to change your request. I really appreciate your helping me out. If you need to trade some days off in the future, I'll be glad to help you."

Fran smiled. "Boy, Deb, I thought this was going to be the end of our friendship. I thought you were going to beg me to trade or threaten me or something. I'm glad it was so easy."

Debra smiled, too. She was busy filling out her request form.

DEALING WITH VIOLENT SITUATIONS

When violence has progressed beyond threats, you have fewer options (you're really down to two: fight or flight). Trying to appease the aggressor or negotiate probably won't work at this point.

If you encounter a situation that looks potentially violent, get out. Situations you're not equipped to handle are those where participants outnumber you, have weapons, or are under the influence of drugs or alcohol. Turnaround and leave. Call for help. This is no time to be a hero.

When a confrontation has not progressed to violence, you can best defuse the situation by calming down the emotions. It's not always helpful to point out the obvious, either. You help people calm down by being calm yourself.

Examine your own behavior for signs of aggressiveness. If you're invading someone else's space, take a step or two back. If you're shouting, lower your voice. If you're pointing your finger, try to adopt a less threatening posture.

Bring your feelings (and the other person's) out into the open. Try to discern and acknowledge feelings. "You sound really angry about that," or "It sounds as if you're pretty upset with me." Then, let the other person talk. When people are given the chance to *talk* about their feelings, they don't have to *act them out*. Talking helps them recognize their emotions and get rid of the feelings safely.

To defuse the situation, however, you have to hear the person out. Most people hear a few words, and then they react to what they are hearing and jump headlong into the argument. Listening is perhaps the most important tool in communication.

When you listen reflectively to a person, you try to understand his point of view. To do that, you have to step out of your own thoughts for the moment and step into his. The worst thing you can say is, "I know just how you feel," because you don't know. All you know is how you would feel in that situation, and that might be far from the way the other person feels.

Listening reflectively usually deescalates conflict. However, if that isn't working (if your adversary isn't willing to share his thoughts or feelings, or doesn't know them himself), watch for nonverbal signs that the conflict is escalating. When a person starts speaking more rapidly, he's usually excited or agitated. Note if he raises his voice. Loudness often occurs with frustration and anger.

The situation is spiraling out of control when the other person adopts these aggressive postures: moving into your territory, shouting in your face, clenching his fists, and tensing his body. Back off and speak more quietly. In order to hear you, the other person has to quiet down himself.

Maintain a sense of humor. That doesn't mean laugh at the other person. Rather, you simply want to lighten the situation, and finding something amusing in it might be a way for you to maintain your poise.

If a confrontation continues to escalate, despite your attempts to listen, understand, and communicate more effectively, you have only two options left: avoid this confrontation or fight. Sometimes there are reasons to fight, but it's far wiser to negotiate.

P A R T ◇ III

USING PEER MEDIATION

CHAPTER ◇ 5

When Do You Need
Peer Mediation?

Melissa and Danielle had been good friends, but in the beginning of tenth grade, things seemed to change. Melissa was on the girls' basketball team and made other friends. People discovered she was as good an athlete as she was a student.

Danielle wasn't interested in playing basketball, although she used to shoot hoops with Melissa on weekends just for fun. Whenever she hung around Melissa and her new friends, she felt in the way. Worse, she felt inferior to them.

Danielle grew bitter and envious, though she didn't actually put these feelings into words. She knew she didn't feel happy for Melissa's popularity, but it seemed petty to be jealous. Gradually, she convinced herself that Melissa was the one to blame.

One day at lunch Danielle arrived too late to sit at the table with Melissa and her friends. Danielle took a seat at

67

a different table. Another girl she knew from history class sat down with her lunch tray.

"Mind if I join you?" she asked.

"No, I'm by myself," Danielle said. "My friends didn't save me a seat today."

The girl glanced over where Danielle was looking. "Aren't you friends with them?" she asked.

"Oh, I don't know," Danielle said, sighing. "I guess sometimes."

"I think those girls are snobs," the other girl said.

And then, without understanding why she'd ever say such a thing, Danielle said, "You know, Melissa and I used to be best friends. That's before she got on the basketball team. I found out she's on drugs. That certainly ended the friendship."

The other girl almost choked on her food. "Melissa is on drugs?" she said.

Danielle cringed. Why had she made up such a story? "Well, I doubt she's going to admit it . . ." Danielle said, glancing over at her unsuspecting friend. "It just goes to show you never know," she added.

"Wow, I can't believe that," the other girl said, and Danielle knew she really did believe it and would be spreading the gossip before the end of lunch.

By the time Melissa heard the stories about her being on drugs, no one was sure who had started the rumor. Danielle squelched her guilty feelings; "Melissa had it coming," she told herself. She started to avoid Melissa, and word spread that Danielle had concocted the story. Melissa and her friends wanted to get even with Danielle. Danielle couldn't believe how the situation had gotten so out of control.

Even though both Danielle and Melissa lacked the skills to work through this conflict, their school had a peer mediation program and student participants who did have problem-solving skills. These peer mediators would be able to show Danielle and Melissa how to solve their conflict.

Mediation comes from the Latin word *mediare*, which means to divide in the middle. A mediator is a person who figuratively jumps into the middle of a conflict and helps the participants solve it. In a mediation, the mediator will help the participants solve the problem themselves. He acts as a role model and referee at times, and does not dictate terms of any agreement.

Students often find it easier to talk to a peer mediator (someone their age) than to an authority figure. They assume (usually correctly) that their peers will understand them better. Peers sometimes are better than adults at getting a fellow student to talk about what's bothering him. Talking to peer mediators (who help *you* solve your problem rather than solve it for you) is probably more comfortable than getting sent to the principal's office or to see the school social worker.

Finally, students learn how to resolve future conflicts by practicing what they've observed in their own peer mediation sessions.

PURPOSE OF PEER MEDIATION

Potential mediators are handpicked from the student body and trained to act as third-party negotiators in resolving conflicts (between students, as well as between students and teachers). Students as young as third graders have successfully learned conflict resolution skills. The good thing about starting training so young is that these students carry their skills with them through high school and ultimately, the rest of their lives.

Some schools offer classes in conflict resolution skills. The students who are interested can go for additional training to serve as peer mediators. In other schools, guidance counselors select certain students to train as peer mediators. They learn the necessary skills in workshops or in conjunction with other agencies.

Qualities of a Peer Mediator

Schools like to have peer mediators with different backgrounds and skills to better match up with the student population. A student in need of a peer mediator will be paired up with someone whose background or personality is most similar to his. Some peer mediators will be honor students; some will be athletes; some will be average students who have special talents. There is no stereotype of the perfect mediator.

However, those students who are best at solving conflicts are good listeners as well as communicators. They understand nonverbal communication and do not attempt to intimidate their peers. They are willing to suspend judgment so that they can hear all sides to a conflict, recognizing that their job is to model good conflict resolution sills, not solve the problem themselves. Listening also means following and encouraging. Some people have a hard time getting the words out. They may need help in finding the right words or to encourage them to keep talking. Good mediators help the person talk by asking him feeling questions, such as "How do you feel about that?" and "What would you like to do about that?"

Peer mediators need to be able to function well without constant supervision, which means exercising good judgment, being resourceful, and having high self-esteem. The resourceful peer mediator tosses out ideas but lets the conflict participants decide themselves what solution will work best for them. This person, then, is both a leader and a follower, depending on the circumstances. Moreover, peer mediators need to be able to keep confidentiality.

WHAT PEER MEDIATORS DO

However they're selected, peer mediators do essentially the same things:

- They work with the students to help them negotiate a nonviolent way out of their conflicts. In the past, many students would settle their disputes out behind the schoolhouse. Now that guns are so accessible, it is even less wise to settle disputes by fighting.
- They help students come to agreement with school officials (teachers and attendance counselors) and thus keep kids from being suspended or sent to the principal's office.
- They teach others (through example) lifelong conflict resolution skills.

Peer mediators (who usually wear identifying pins or shirts) are always available to help settle disputes. Sometimes they're called upon to talk with students during school hours (a study hall or lunch break); other times, they arrange a later appointment with the student.

CONFLICTS HANDLED BY PEER MEDIATORS

Technically, peer mediators handle disputes arising from disagreements between students, poor attendance, and trouble between teacher and student. In the latter event, peer mediators will be paired with an adult mediator because of the teacher's involvement.

Peer mediators/counselors handle:

1) *Conflicts between students*, including students who gossip about each other, students who have stopped being friends with each other or who actively try to break up new relationships, students who borrow things and either don't return them or return them in worse shape than they received them, and students who bully others or are bullied.

2) *Conflicts between teacher and student* resulting from poor classroom attendance, poor grades, or antagonism between the two parties.

3) *Conflicts about family problems*, including worries over an impending divorce, fears about moving (or having just moved), difficulties getting along with siblings or stepsiblings, and poor communication with parents.

Peer mediators do not handle physically violent confrontations.

Peer mediators *refer to a professional*:

1) Any student who is abusing drugs or alcohol (or whose family is abusing drugs or alcohol).

2) Any student who reports physical or sexual abuse in his or her family. The peer mediator is obligated by law to report instances of physical and sexual abuse. He or she usually reports first to his peer advisor and then to the police or Department of Human Services/Child Protective Services.

3) Any student who is pregnant (because she needs prenatal care or advice concerning the pregnancy).

4) Any student expressing suicidal thoughts. A peer mediator/counselor is not trained to deal with life-and-death situations, and it is not up to him or her to determine if a student is genuinely suicidal.

5) Any student who appears to be suffering from an emotional disorder. A student mediator lacks the experience or skills to deal with mental disorders.

Even though a peer mediator refers a student to a professional for help, that doesn't mean he or she has nothing further to do with the student. Support can still be offered to the student who might otherwise remain in school feeling awkward and alone.

GROUND RULES FOR MEDIATION

The peer mediator wants to make the ground rules very clear when she sits down with students. For mediation to work, the participants have to agree to certain stipulations.

1) Both sides agree to listen to each other. No interrupting or name-calling.

2) Both sides agree to work together on a solution.
3) Both sides (as well as the mediator herself) agree to keep what transpired in their meeting confidential.

CHAPTER 6

What Happens in a Peer Mediation Session?

I f Melissa and Danielle didn't happen to attend a school that had a peer mediation program, there wouldn't be many options for them to resolve their conflict. Melissa is justifiably outraged that Danielle would spread such a rumor about her around school. Her friends have thought of retaliating with a few rumors of their own. The classroom is filled with tension whenever the two of them are together.

Melissa comes from a family that doesn't like to talk about its problems. Her father's motto is "Don't make waves." It's no wonder, then, that Melissa views conflict negatively and hasn't much of a clue as to how to confront someone and attempt to discuss the problem. She's been raised to hope conflict will go away on its own.

Danielle comes from a family that views apologies as a sign of weakness. She knows she owes Melissa an apology, but she just can't bring herself to say the words. Besides, she isn't sure how much Melissa cares about the whole situation. Melissa isn't the one who's fuming in public; it's her friends. Melissa is just ignoring her, and two can play that game, thinks Danielle.

What are the chances that this conflict will ever get satisfactorily resolved?

Fortunately, the girls attend a high school that does have a peer mediation program. Melissa fumes in private about the rumors, and the tension in the classroom grows. One day the teacher pairs Melissa and Danielle for a project, and they refuse to work together. The teacher is shocked at their behavior. Melissa and Danielle had never given her problems before. Then another student lets the teacher in on the situation. The teacher takes Melissa and Danielle aside. "Why don't you two talk about the situation and work it out," she suggests.

Melissa stares at Danielle. "There's nothing to work out. I'm not the one who did anything wrong."

"Are you saying I'm to blame?" Danielle countered.

"Well, you're the one who started the rumors . . ."

"You don't know that," Danielle said.

"Look, I don't care what goes on as long as I don't have to work with Danielle on any project. I don't feel like working with her."

"No big deal," Danielle said. 'You haven't felt like doing anything with me for a long time."

The teacher interrupted them. "This is going nowhere," she said. "I think you two ought to work this out with a peer mediator."

"Oh, give me a break," Danielle said.

"No, I'm serious," the teacher said. "Why not give it a try?"

"I'm not talking about my problems in front of some other kid," Melissa said.

"Why not? These students have learned how to problem-solve. Looks to me like you two could use some training yourself."

"I think the idea's crazy," Melissa said.

"I'll go if she goes," Danielle said.

"We're taking up too much class time discussing this," the teacher said. "Think about it, and talk to me after class."

The girls returned to their seats. Melissa was more embarrassed than ever. It was bad enough what Danielle had said about her, but now she had to go get counseling because of it. Would this humiliation ever end?

Danielle sent her a note. "I'll go if you go," it said.

By class's end, Melissa figured she might as well take the teacher up on her suggestion. But she wasn't looking forward to it.

She and Danielle agreed to talk over their problem with a peer mediator the next day after school. Both girls arrived a few minutes after 2:30 in the guidance office. A few minutes later, another girl came bustling into the office.

"I'm sorry I'm late," she announced, and it was only then that Melissa and Danielle figured out she was the peer mediator.

"I'm Karyn," the girl said, extending her hand. "You must be Melissa; I've seen you play basketball. And you must be Danielle."

"This isn't our idea," Danielle said, not knowing why she chose that as the first thing to say.

"Why don't we go to the cafeteria and talk about this," Karyn said. "It won't feel so official."

"Okay," Danielle said. "But we're not really sold on this peer mediating thing."

Karyn picked a secluded spot in the back of the cafeteria. She brought Melissa and Danielle sodas and sat down with them at one of the tables. "Let me tell you about peer mediation," she said. "I've been through conflict resolution training. It doesn't mean I'm a great student; it just means I know how to work through problems. My job here as I see it is to help you two solve your conflict. The ground rules are simple. No name calling, and no interrupting each other. You both agree to listen to each other."

"Okay," Danielle mumbled.

"Sure," Melissa said.

"So, Melissa, why don't you tell me what the problem is?"

Melissa looked surprised. "Why don't you ask Danielle first."

Danielle was busy looking at her soda.

"It doesn't matter who starts," Karyn said. "Both of you will get time to describe the problem."

"This feels really stupid," Melissa said. "I don't think it's worth talking about."

"Why is that?" Karyn asked.

"Because it's no big deal."

"But you agreed to talk about this," Karyn said.

"Okay, okay. But it sounds stupid." She sighed and then looked over at Danielle. "I guess the problem is Danielle has been spreading rumors that I'm on drugs." She smiled weakly at Karyn. "I told you it was stupid."

Karyn raised an eyebrow. "Spreading rumors isn't very kind," she said. "How do you know she's doing that?"

Danielle sat looking at her hands.

"Because I've heard the rumors, and people say that Danielle started them."

Karyn looked at Danielle. "Is that true?" she asked.

"Well, sort of," Danielle said.

"What do you mean?"

"Okay, so I made up some stuff. Big deal. It was a joke."

"A joke?" Melissa shouted. "I don't think saying someone is on drugs is very funny."

"It was a joke."

"What prompted you to say that about Melissa?" Karyn asked.

"I don't know. I guess I felt like hurting her."

"Hurting me? What for?" Melissa said.

"Please let each other finish what she's saying," Karyn said.

"She had all the friends," Danielle said, looking at Karyn.

"Tell me how that made you feel?" Karyn asked.

"Left out," Danielle said. "Melissa never had time for me anymore."

"Were you aware Danielle felt this way?" Karyn asked.

Melissa looked surprised. "I still spent time with you," Melissa said. "I just have a lot of activities."

"You didn't answer my question," Karyn said.

"No," Melissa said. "I guess I didn't know that."

"Did you try to tell Melissa how you were feeling?" Karyn asked Danielle.

"She could tell," Danielle said.

"How was I supposed to know you were feeling left out?" Melissa said.

"You should have noticed that I wasn't around much anymore," Danielle said.

"Well, I thought that's because you didn't like my friends. How was I supposed to know you were feeling left out?"

"You're supposed to be smart."

"Let's not get into blaming each other. That doesn't help us figure things out. Melissa, what I'm hearing you say is that you are upset because Danielle was spreading rumors about you being on drugs.

"And Danielle, you're admitting you spread the rumors, but you did it because you were feeling left out, and I assume, angry."

"I wasn't angry; I was hurt," Danielle said.

"Well, that was a pretty mean thing to do," Melissa said.

"I was feeling mean," Danielle said. She looked at Karyn. "Melissa and I used to do everything together. This year she gets on the basketball team and everything changes. Now she doesn't have any time for me."

"You could have tried out for the basketball team," Melissa said.

"I wouldn't have made it; I'm not that good. Besides, I'd rather watch it."

"Well, there are other things we could do," Melissa offered.

"I got the feeling you were too busy with your other friends."

"What made you think that?" Melissa said.

"You're hanging out with the popular kids," Danielle said.

"Well, you could, too," Melissa said.

"Wait a minute," Karyn said. "Can you each tell me what the problem is from the other person's perspective?"

"Melissa doesn't know how I feel. She thinks it's easy making new friends," Danielle said.

"That's how *you* see it," Karyn said. "Tell me what Melissa thinks about the situation."

"She thinks I'm being a jerk."

"Did she say that?"

"Not in so many words," Danielle said.

"Oh, come on," Melissa said. "I think you misunderstood the situation. You seem to think I've ditched you for my basketball friends. But I haven't been any different."

"Tell me how Danielle has said she feels," Karyn said.

"She says she feels left out," Melissa said. She looked at Danielle. "I'm sorry you felt that way. I didn't think much about it. Maybe I was caught up in my own popularity."

Danielle looked at Melissa. "You don't need to apologize; I do. I'm the one who made up those awful stories."

"If the problem was a misunderstanding between the two of you, how can you fix it?" Karyn asked.

"I can apologize," Danielle offered.

"It's okay," Melissa said. "Next time, though, tell me what's bothering you. I didn't know you felt so left out."

"I guess it would have been easier," Danielle said. "I just thought I was being petty."

"Well, I thought if I ignored you long enough, the whole thing would blow over," Melissa said.

"It sounds like you both needed to air your feelings. Is there anything else you need to talk about?" Karyn asked.

"Oh, I don't know," Melissa said. "Danielle, do you want to still work on that English project?"

BECOMING A PEER MEDIATOR

If you're interested in becoming a peer mediator, check out what's available in the way of training at your school. Some schools offer classes for students; some send volunteers to conflict resolution workshops. If your school does not have any program in place, you can help get one started.

Talk to your guidance counselors first or the school social workers. They should know how to get information on starting a peer mediation program. If they do not, you can write to the New Mexico Center for Dispute Resolution or the National Institute for Dispute Resolution, which are listed in the "Where to Go for Help" section of this book.

RESULTS OF PEER MEDIATION PROGRAMS

Peer mediation programs reduce cases of vandalism in schools, school violence, and chronic absenteeism. They encourage students to take responsibility for solving their own conflicts, and allow teachers to devote more time to teaching, rather than to discipline. Furthermore, these programs result in improved communication in general between students, and students and adults. Mediation training offers students communication and listening skills that are useful in all areas of their lives.

Conclusion: Affecting the Outcome

If you recall the conflict continuum, you'll remember that the more you rely on a third party to settle your conflicts, the less effect you have over the outcome. Negotiating conflicts yourself allows you to share in the choice of a solution.

Mediation introduces a neutral third party who can guide you in your conflict resolution. By the time you've agreed to arbitration or litigation, the solution is out of your hands. Both arbitration and the courts are the last stages in conflict resolution. In each case, a third party (whether an arbitrator, a judge, or a jury) has the authority to settle the dispute, and his or her decision is binding. Arbitrators are employed by the courts to handle cases that can be resolved without litigation. When you give your case to an arbitrator, however, you give up the chance to negotiate on your own.

When you litigate, negotiation is no longer the issue; it's whose side is legally right.

THE LITIGATION MENTALITY

Once you go to court, whether you use lawyers or represent yourself, a litigation mentality develops. Both sides, naturally wanting to win, turn into adversaries. Both will probably become attached to their points of view. In order for one side to win, the other side has to lose.

Lawyers are trained to win cases. When winning is your main goal, you resort to any tactic that will increase your chances. That means being aggressive (with both witnesses and your adversary) and discrediting the other side. These procedures are all designed to destroy relationships. Furthermore, lawyers often ask for more money than you can afford.

ADVANTAGES

1) The main advantage to suing is also its main disadvantage: it's out of your hands. If you are not assertive enough to practice good negotiating skills on your own, you can give your case to an arbitrator (or the courts), who can decide the outcome for you. Furthermore, you don't have to feel like the bad guy (if that's a problem for you). You don't have to come up with the solution that meets everyone's needs, so the pressure to be objective and creative is off.

2) When negotiation fails, arbitration (or litigation) is better than giving up. Even if you only have a small chance of winning, by promising to take your case to court, you can sometimes force the other side into a settlement (which is actually forced negotiation).

When you have a conflict, and the other side refuses to cooperate in seeking a mutually satisfying solution, you're bound to feel angry and frustrated. Seeking redress through the courts is a final way of asserting your needs.

3) Arbitration or litigation may be your only way of fulfilling your needs. Some people always refuse to negotiate. They may think that if they ignore your grievance, it will go away (along with you). Other people may think

that because you have a good relationship with them, you'll tolerate a few conflicts to preserve the relationship. Ironically, they're harming the relationship themselves by minimizing the conflict instead of addressing it. In these situations, you'll never get any conflicts resolved if you don't make them official (by handing them over to the courts to resolve).

4) You stand a good chance of getting your conflict resolved. An arbitrator *will* make a decision, just as the courts will make some kind of decision (either suggesting mediation or rendering a decision themselves). Negotiations can always grind to a standstill, but the courts will not. Of course, the decision may not be what you hoped for, but at least you won't be in limbo.

DISADVANTAGES

1) Again, the fact that the whole matter is out of your hands may be considered an advantage or a disadvantage. If you want a role in hammering out the solution, you're going to be frustrated; the arbitrator, judge, or jury will handle that. If you don't like the decision, as a rule, there's not much you can do about it.

2) Both parties are immediately identified as adversaries. If you have a good relationship with the other party, litigation usually hurts that relationship. Both sides adopt the win/lose mentality, and both (naturally) want to be the winner. To be the winner, you sometimes have to resort to dirty tactics (none of which will endear you to the other side). And even if you win, there's a price to pay: You will probably have antagonized the losing side and ruined the relationship.

3) It costs money to go to court. If you win, it may well be worth the money spent (or your lawyer may recoup your losses). If you lose, you not only end up dissatisfied, you have to pay court costs and your lawyer's fee. It can be quite expensive to try your case in court.

4) Once a decision is rendered, there's nothing else you can do. If the decision doesn't go in your favor, you're certainly not likely to get your opponent to return to the negotiating table. You're left with strong feelings about the loss, and no recourse.

LOSING THE CASE

Marshall Emory worked one summer with his father, who did carpentry work on a small scale. Together they constructed a storage building for a local grocer. In their contract, the grocer agreed to pay Marshall and his dad for labor and the cost of materials (upon satisfaction). After the building was finished, the grocer claimed it leaked and that as a result, "he wasn't satisfied" and wouldn't reimburse them for labor or materials.

Marshall needed the money because he was saving to buy a car. His father wasn't in a position to pay him if he wasn't paid himself. Furthermore, Marshall's dad had borrowed money to purchase $1,000 worth of materials; at the very least, he wanted to be reimbursed for their cost.

Mr. Emory appealed to the grocer to sit down and negotiate this conflict. Was there any way he and Marshall could salvage the situation?

The grocer (who may have wanted a storage building for free) refused to negotiate. He reminded them of the terms of the contract, which were quite explicit: payment upon satisfaction, and the grocer wasn't satisfied. At first, he gave Mr. Emory and Marshall the chance to fix the building, but the more they worked on it, the more fault the grocer found with their efforts. Finally, the grocer threw up his hands.

"You can't fix it, so forget it," he said.

"But you still owe us for the building materials."

"No, I don't. The contract is very specific. If I'm not satisfied, I don't have to pay a thing."

Technically, the grocer was right. He didn't have to pay anything; it would have been "the right thing to do" to preserve a relationship with Marshall and his dad, but apparently the grocer didn't care about that.

Marshall wanted to dismantle the storage building in the middle of the night, but his dad feared the grocer would call the police on them. Their only other choice was to take the grocer to court.

Justice was swift, though hardly "just." The grocer, who showed a copy of his contract to the court, won the decision. He did not have to pay for the building, and Marshall and his dad would not recoup their losses.

Marshall was furious. He had invested a lot of time in that building, and now his dad couldn't pay him because he had to use his own money to pay off the loan on the materials. It would be a long time before Marshall could get that car. He fumed and thought of nothing else. He plotted revenge.

Mr. Emory took a different approach. Recognizing that they'd lost the case (even though he didn't agree with the judge's decision), he knew he had to put the experience behind him. He had to let it go. He couldn't get his materials back or get paid for his labor, but he could stop patronizing the grocery store and could even encourage his friends to boycott it as well. Also, he could figure out the lesson in all of this.

When you lose the case in court or an arbitrator decides against you, you have to let go of your feelings of anger and revenge. Legally, there is nothing more you can do. Letting go doesn't mean telling yourself it doesn't matter. Of course it matters. That's why you're so mad. However, hanging onto all that anger will only poison you. Better to have learned from the experience so that you can avoid a similar controversy in the future.

You can be mad for a few days, or you can be mad for the rest of your life. If you let the bad experience ruin your life, though, you've given a lot of power to your adversary. Sometimes, judges and juries don't make fair decisions; after all, they are human. When a ruling doesn't seem fair (and it's not necessarily unfair just because it doesn't go in your favor), you can do three things:

Let go of the anger, for that only ties you to your adversary. Learn from the experience. Decide what you can do to protect yourself from further conflict with this party. In Marshall's case, they stopped shopping at that grocery store, and they filed a note with the Better Business Bureau. Having done that, they got on with their lives.

Arbitration and litigation should be the last steps you take in resolving a conflict, since they are both costly and probably damaging to your relationship with the other party. Besides, it's better for your self-esteem to negotiate your own settlement. If you use the skills you learned in this book toward the conflicts you encounter, you can make the best decisions for handling them wisely.

Glossary

Aggressive   Invading someone else's space; not respecting boundaries.

Arbitration   Using a third-party negotiator who has the legal authority to settle the disputants' conflict.

Assertive   Clearly stating your needs without crossing others' boundaries, while at the same time respecting your own.

Attending   Paying close attention to someone, looking at him as you listen to him talk.

Barriers to communication   Types of behavior that escalate a conflict (specifically: name-calling, threatening, moralizing, advising, and diverting).

Collaboration   Sitting down with your partner to arrive at a thorough examination of the problem, utilizing options that will help all parties satisfy their needs.

Compromise   To settle for half as much as you want.

Conflict partnership   Two opponents in a conflict with the mutual goal of working to satisfy both parties' needs.

Congruent   When the outward expression of your feelings matches *how* you're feeling.

Empathize   To understand another person's experiences.

Interpersonal   Between yourself and others.

Intrapersonal   Within yourself.

Mediation   Using an unbiased third party negotiator to help disputants resolve their conflict.

Pressure tactics   Ways of acting nonviolently (specifically: using strikes, boycotts, protests, and fasts) to draw attention to your cause and to block your adversary's actions.

Reflective listening   Listening to a person in order to understand his experience through his eyes, then reflecting it back
to him in your own words.

Where to Go for Help

INFORMATION

National Institute for Dispute Resolution
1726 M St. NW
Suite 500
Washington, DC 20036
(202) 466-4767

New Mexico Center for Dispute Resolution
800 Park Ave. SW
Albuquerque, NM 87102
(505) 247-0571

WEB SITES

Conflict Resolution/Peer Mediation Links
http://www.coe.ufl.edu/CRPM/othersites.htm/

Institute for Global Communications (IGC)
http://www.conflictnet.org/igc

Resolving Conflict Creatively Program
http://www.benjerry.com/esr/index.htm/

For Further Reading

Ayres, Alex (ed.). *The Wisdom of Martin Luther King, Jr.* New York: Penguin Books, 1993.

Bazerman, Max. *Negotiating Rationally.* New York: The Free Press, 1992.

Brinkman, Dr. Rick, and Kirschner, Dr. Rick. *Dealing with People You Can't Stand.* New York: McGraw-Hill, 1994.

Carter, Jimmy. *Talking Peace.* New York: Dutton Children's Books, 1993.

Covey, Stephen. *The Seven Habits of Highly Effective People.* New York: Simon & Schuster, 1989.

Crum, Thomas. *The Magic of Conflict.* New York: Simon & Schuster, 1987.

Dalton, Dennis. *Mahatma Gandhi. Nonviolent Power in Action.* New York: Columbia Press, 1993.

Edelman, Joel, and Crain, Mary Beth. *The Tao of Negotiation.* New York: HarperCollins, 1994.

Fisher, Roger, and Ury, William. *Getting to Yes.* New York: Penguin Books, 1983.

Freund, James C. *Smart Negotiating.* New York: Simon & Schuster, 1992.

Hocker, Joyce, and Wilmost, William. *Interpersonal Conflict.* USA: Wm. C. Brown Communications, Inc., 1995.

Jandt, Fred. *Win–Win Negotiating.* New York: John Wiley & Sons, 1985.

Kennedy, Gavin. *The Perfect Negotiation.* New York: Wings Books, 1992.

Pollan, Stephen, and Levine, Mark. *The Total Negotiator.* New York: Avon Books, 1994.

Reck, Ross, and Long, Brian. *The Win-Win Negotiator*. New York: Pocket Books, 1987.

Sherrow, Victoria. *Mohandas Gandhi*. Brookfield, CT: The Millbrook Press, 1994.

Walton, Donald. *Are You Communicating?* New York: McGraw-Hill, 1989.

Watley, William. *Roots of Resistance*. Valley Forge, PA: Judson Press, 1985.

Weeks, Dudley. *The Eight Essential Steps to Conflict Resolution*. New York: G.P. Putnam's Sons, 1992.

Weisbrot, Robert. *Marching Toward Freedom*. New York: Chelsea House, 1994.

Index

A

active listening techniques,
32–33
alcohol abuse, 72
anger, 28–29, 42
apologizing, 41
arbitration
advantages of, 84–85
defined, 3, 83
disadvantages of, 85–86
assertiveness, 35

B

behavior, styles of, 35

C

civil rights movement, 19,
23–25
"clouding," 49, 50
Cold War, 18
communication
in problem-solving, 40–41
skills, 2, 31, 34–39
style, 10

conflict
accommodation in handling,
13–14
and aggression, 14
avoiding, 10–12, 49, 50,
63–65
brainstorming solutions to,
41–42, 61
collaborating to resolve,
15–16
communicating to resolve,
40–41, 64
and compromise, 15
consequences of, 6, 7, 17
defined, 1
denial of, 12–13
displacing, 12
elements of, 9
identifying a problem, 40
in families, 7
on the job, 7–8
"partners" in, 44
three bases for, 2, 7
types of, 8

ways people handle, 10–16
conflict resolution
  defined, 2
  flexibility in, 29
  skills needed, 2, 3, 31, 33
  steps in, 47
  through litigation, 83–88
conflicting psychological needs, 2
conflicting resources, 2
conflicting values, 2
courts, 3, 83

D
drug abuse, 72

E
empathy, 32

F
family, conflict in a, 7
feedback, 39
feelings
  connection with conflict, 29
  recognizing, 28–29
"fogging," 50–51, 52

G
Gandhi, Mahatma, 19–22

I
"I" messages, 34–35

K
King, Martin Luther, 22–25

L
lifestyles, 9
listening skills, 30, 31–32
litigation, 83–84

advantages of, 84–85
disadvantages of, 85–86

M
mediation, 3, 69
mediator, 69
Middle East conflict, 7

N
negotiating, 55–63
  identifying needs in, 56–57, 58
  on the job, 55–56
  steps in, 56–57, 61
  unfair tactics in, 59–60
nonviolent tactics
  used by Mahatma Gandhi, 19, 20, 21, 22
  used by Martin Luther King, 22, 25
  used to protest Vietnam conflict, 19
nuclear threat, 18–19

P
passive-aggressive
  behavior, 36, 38, 55
  defined, 53–54
peace movement, 18–19
peer mediation
  confidentiality in, 71, 74
  defined, 3
  ground rules for, 73–74
  programs in schools, 4, 69, 70
  results of, 82
  sample session, 75–81
peer mediator
  defined, 69
  how to become a, 81–82

qualities of a, 70–71
responsibilities of a, 71
types of conflicts handled by
    a, 72
types of conflicts not
    handled by a, 72–73
physical abuse, 73
power, 43
problem-solving skills, 28–43,
    61
professional help, 72–73

R
"reflecting," 32, 40, 46, 61, 64

S
sexual abuse, 73
stereotypes, 9

V
validating, 33
Vietnam conflict, 19
violence, dealing with, 63–65